General editor: Graham Handle

Brodie's Notes on
The Diary of Anne Frank

Nigel Grant B.Ed. MA
English teacher, St John Fisher RC Comprehensive School, Chatham, Kent

Pan Books London, Sydney and Auckland

First published 1991 by
Pan Books Ltd, Cavaye Place, London sw10 9pg

9 8 7 6 5 4 3 2 1

© Pan Books Ltd 1991

ISBN 0 330 50322 7

Photoset by Parker Typesetting Service, Leicester

Printed and bound in Great Britain by
Clays Ltd, St Ives plc, Bungay, Suffolk

Contents

Page references in these Notes are to the Pan
edition of the *Diary*, but references
are also given to specific dates, so that
the Notes may be used with any edition of the book.

Preface

The intention throughout this study aid is to stimulate and guide, to encourage your involvement in the book, and to develop informed responses and a sure understanding of the main details.

Brodie's Notes provide a clear outline of the play or novel's plot, followed by act, scene, or chapter summaries and/or commentaries. These are designed to emphasize the most important literary and factual details. Poems, stories or non-fiction texts combine brief summary with critical commentary on individual aspects or common features of the genre being examined. Textual notes define what is difficult or obscure and emphasize literary qualities. Revision questions are set at appropriate points to test your ability to appreciate the prescribed book and to write accurately and relevantly about it.

In addition, each of these Notes includes a critical appreciation of the author's art. This covers such major elements as characterization, style, structure, setting and themes. Poems are examined technically – rhyme, rhythm, for instance. In fact, any important aspect of the prescribed work will be evaluated. The aim is to send you back to the text you are studying.

Each study aid concludes with a series of general questions which require a detailed knowledge of the book: some of these questions may invite comparison with other books, some will be suitable for coursework exercises, and some could be adapted to work you are doing on another book or books. Each study aid has been adapted to meet the needs of the current examination requirements. They provide a basic, individual and imaginative response to the work being studied, and it is hoped that they will stimulate you to acquire disciplined reading habits and critical fluency.

Graham Handley 1991

The author and her work

Introduction

There are many reasons why *The Diary of Anne Frank* has been so widely read and highly acclaimed since it was first published in 1947, three years after Anne's death at the age of fifteen. It is honest, funny, revealing, disturbing and, ultimately, tragic. As a testament of the human spirit's ability to transcend injustice, danger and oppression, it has an enduringly wide appeal – to children, to adolescents, to adults, to the Dutch, to the Jews, to all oppressed people. Although it is an individual, personal response to an appalling situation, it also speaks paradoxically in a universal language of hope and determination to overcome all obstacles.

Without such a book and the many insights it gives, our understanding of the disgrace and evil of racial discrimination, embodied in the unimaginable atrocities of the Holocaust, would be greatly impoverished.

The story of the two Jewish families, together with a married man separated from his wife by the war, all of whom are imprisoned for two years in rooms above an old warehouse in Amsterdam to escape the ravages of Nazi anti-Semitism, chronicles the fears and tensions provoked by the savage and unjust discrimination against European Jews. It reveals too the developing genius of a gifted young writer, caught in the naturally difficult years of early adolescence in a fraught, and at times, impossibly claustrophobic situation. Anne's voice becomes the voice of all young people who question imposed adult wisdom and who try to find a sense of their own worth and of what is worthwhile in life, often by a painful process of self-discovery.

The form, style and autobiographical nature of the *Diary* raise some problems as far as literary study is concerned. For example, it does not break into conveniently pre-arranged chapters of continuous narrative. Although there are changes of emphasis and subject matter, the *Diary* tends to move in circles, returning to situations and themes which have been discussed before. At times, the recapitulation casts fresh light on an issue, while at others it simply responds to and records the latest expression of a recurrent situation. Because of this structure I decided to divide the *Diary* into twelve sections, most of which are about twenty pages long. The sections stop at convenient points which indicate a change of mood or of focus in the text. The divisions are often arbitrary, but they result in manageable areas for teaching and study.

Another difficulty is created by the sheer variety of subject matter that Anne provided – simple, spontaneous, chatty information about herself, her school and her friends; war news; deeply introspective examinations of her own nature; reflections on the boy who in some ways became like a lover; critical accounts of the adults who in her eyes often made life unnecessarily difficult. The length and frequency of the letters vary enormously; some are devoted to a single topic while others move swiftly from deeply personal matters to the wider stage of World War II.

As the *Diary* is effectively an autobiography presented in the form of letters, there are references to the Franks' background which it would be unsatisfactory to cover in a fragmented glossary. The following part of the introduction is therefore devoted to a brief history of the family, their origins, and the international situation which caused them to spend two years of confinement above Mr Frank's business premises.

Historical and family background

It is obviously impossible to isolate the personal situation of the Franks, the Van Daans and Albert Dussel from the political context of European Jews in the 1930s and 1940s.

The fundamental starting point was Adolf Hitler, the man who became the German Chancellor, and self-proclaimed President of the Reich, under whose leadership some six million Jews in Germany and other European countries were exterminated in what is now known as the Holocaust.

Hitler's intense hatred of the Jews partly stemmed from Germany's defeat in World War I, which was ascribed irrationally by the Nazis to the Jews. His autobiography *Mein Kampf* ('My Struggle'), promoted hostility against Jews, which ranged in expression from beatings and destruction of careers to fully fledged genocide ('the murder of a race') as his army ranged aggressively across Europe in the cause of Aryan imperialism.

Read in Tony Bayfield's *Churban* about the Kristallnacht ('Crystal Night') of 10 November 1938, when anti-Semitism in Germany exploded into a terrifying demonstration of Nazi malice and cruelty.

Otto Frank, Anne's father, was a German Jew who had decided to leave his home in Frankfort-am-Main in 1933 to escape the accelerating anti-Semitism apparent in his country. He came from a family of bankers, but professional difficulties forced him into a new career in Amsterdam with the firm of Travies & Co. selling domestic grocery products. His wife, Edith, and their two daughters, Margot Betti and Anneliese Marie, soon followed him and they settled to their new, safe life in Holland. Both Otto and Edith had come from privileged, cultured backgrounds, a point that is important to bear in mind as we read about how they later coped with the conditions of their hidden life in the 'Secret Annexe' above his firm's warehouse. An awareness of the conditions that Anne describes so vividly is also necessary if we are to appreciate the quality and range of Anne's and Margot's thoughts and interests as they remained imprisoned for two years of their adolescence.

The security of their new life came to an end on Friday 10 May 1940, when Holland was invaded by Germany – the conquest was completed within five days. By the autumn of 1940, Dutch Jews were beginning to feel the force of German racial oppression, later symbolized clearly in the yellow six-pointed star which all Jews were forced early in 1942 to sew on the breast of their clothes; they were also forced to write *Jood* ('Jew') on the star as a further sign of their racial alienation.

Otto Frank responded swiftly to the danger that now threatened his family and colleagues. He officially resigned as managing director of Travies & Co. and substituted a Christian friend, Mr Koophuis, thus shielding his colleagues from any German accusations that they were conniving with Jews. He then decided in the spring of 1942 to go into hiding, a move precipitated early in July by receiving a 'call-up' for his older daughter Margot from the German authorities. The term 'call-up' was of course a euphemism for imprisonment, and very possibly torture and death. With the help of their friends Miep and Henk Van Senten, they immediately left their comfortable home in the suburbs of Amsterdam and hid in the empty room above the firm's warehouse at 263 Prinsengracht.

Although the premises were adequate for a family of four, the situation soon changed when Herman Van Daan (a colleague of Otto Frank), his wife Petronella, their teenage son Peter and, later, a Jewish dentist, Friedrich Dussel, also sought asylum with the Franks in what Anne called *Achterhuis* (their 'room behind' or 'Secret Annexe'). Eight people were now cramped into the upper floors of an old building, sharing washing, toilet and sleeping facilities *for two years without ever leaving the building*. They had to remain virtually silent during working hours from Mondays to Fridays every week so that the Travies' staff beneath who did not know of their secret remained ignorant of their presence. The strain must have been enormous, and as Anne's diary clearly shows, it led to frequent displays of temper and tension within the group.

When seen in the light of these difficult and trying circumstances the diary is all the more astonishing for its humour, tolerance and general absence of self-pity. It is a remarkable book, bred out of an extreme situation, and exhibits very clearly the hallmark of a born writer whose facility with words was due partly to the extent of her reading, but also to the power and insight of an unusually lively, generous and adventurous mind. The maturity of her perceptions of herself and those around her is no less arresting than the confident, lucid style in which they are presented. The range of her subject matter is effortlessly covered, so that we receive a rounded, living portrait of a literate, sensitive, popular, cheeky, witty girl, bubbling over with fun and charm, who is yet an intensely private and reflective young woman.

The later years of her short life were spent striving to find an inner peace, the elusiveness and rewards of which she describes so eloquently. The need to find acceptance and understanding from her family and friends is a major force behind this search and prompts some uncannily lucid and revealing insights. Her diary assures her of the recognition that she clearly sought from all around her. Her tragedy is that she never lived to rejoice in it.

Summary and textual background

The Diary of Anne Frank comprises one hundred and seventy three entries from Sunday 14 June 1942, two days after Anne's thirteenth birthday, to Tuesday 1 August 1944, three days before the Franks, Van Daans and Dussel were captured at their sanctuary.

Although there are sections of consecutive daily entries, there are other times when several days and even weeks pass without mention. There are two reasons for this. Firstly, the Pan edition of the *Diary* used as the basis for this study is a British translation from the Dutch. The complete diary, which Anne revised with a view to publication and which was edited by her father after her death, is available in the critical edition listed in the bibliography at the end of these notes. It was decided to abridge Anne's work as it contained references to third parties who might have been embarrassed by having their names made public. Explicit sexual references were cut out, as were personal comments about Anne's mother and the Van Daans.

Secondly, Anne seemed to write when she really wanted to say something, however brief. There is no sense of a futile resolution to enter mechanically a daily statement, but rather the feeling that she waits for an appropriate moment to express her thoughts and feelings (see the entry for 20 July 1942). The occasional lack of chronological continuity can thus be seen simply as Anne's creative exercise of choice and judgement.

The diary form permits a number of features impossible in a more disciplined genre. It allows the writer to move uninhibitedly between widely varied subject matter in the one entry and we frequently see references to the war, her parents, the Van Daans and Peter tumbling naturally onto the page as she turns her attention to them in turn.

It also establishes an intimate bond between writer and reader, probably unintentional at first, which reflects the natural sense of audience so apparent in Anne's work. The informality created by the imaginative device of giving a diary a name, 'Dear Kitty', rather than the more common 'Dear Diary', establishes intimacy, and at the same time heightens our awareness of the need of an emotionally isolated girl to create a surrogate friend with whom she can share her innermost thoughts and feelings, whether about her attitude to herself, her family, her ideals or her young lover.

The bulk of the diary was written in the second year of the group's confinement. In this second larger section, Anne's thoughts about her own aspirations, her changing feelings about Peter and her growing insights into her relationship with her parents tend to supplant the smaller concerns of day to day events which feature largely in the first half. This is entirely natural; she is growing older, surrounded by adults, and spends a great deal of time in study. She changes very noticeably from a high-spirited child into a reflective, earnest young woman, with an independent and original mind. She achieves this however without losing her liveliness and sense of what is right. It is a very definite change, and yet there is always time for the odd wry comment or description of a humorous scene drawn from observation of their daily routine.

One marked feature of the latter half of the book is the increased attention Anne gives to war developments. She becomes of an age to recognize the validity of political matters and lives in growing excited hope of the liberation of Holland that she never lived to see. This war news is always more than mere factual reportage. Events of international importance come alive for us as we see their direct effect on the inhabitants of the *achterhuis*. This personal account of the effects of the war is combined with Anne's perceptive and controlled insights into her relationships with others. At all times the diary is a joy to read – clear, sincere, often profound, vigorous and entertaining. From it we receive an evocative picture of three main subjects: an individual triumphing over the trial of adolescence in a forced, potentially destructive environment, a group of frightened Jews determined to escape the anti-Semitic purges of German Nazism and a defenceless country struggling against occupation by an evil foreign power.

Section summaries, critical commentary and textual notes

Section 1 14 June 1942–5 July 1942

Although the commentary will focus on sections rather than individual letters, the dedication and the first entry reveal much that is very relevant to the book as a whole.

The dedication is far removed from a run-of-the mill intention to keep a diary. The language is solemn – 'confide, support' – and the directness of the statement absolves it from any accusation of self-pity. Clearly, Anne feels herself to be emotionally alone and there is considerable pathos in this thirteen-year-old's dignified vision of her own loneliness and wish for companionship. To be able to write with such conviction immediately identifies her as an unusual child whose writing suggests levels of originality and imaginative force far beyond the norm.

The first real entry is remarkable for two things: firstly, the fresh, natural, conversational style of the opening 'no wonder . . .' Details accumulate and are punctuated by comments about herself and her birthday presents, addressed directly to the diary. She injects the description with vitality and delight, re-creating scenes and feelings vividly and enthusiastically. As well as sweets and toys, books feature largely among her presents and she plans to buy a book of Graeco-Roman mythology. She obviously loves imaginative stories and revels in the opportunity to extend the range of her reading.

With the exception of the letter of 20 July, the rest of this section is about the sorts of things that are not unusual for a girl of her age – friends, a birthday party, boys, school. She is relaxed, cheerful and within the limitations placed upon her by German anti-Jewish restrictions, leads a happy, normal life relatively untouched by the fact that she is a member of a race despised by the occupying power in her country. If we look for example at her relationship with Harry Goldberg (pp. 19–21), Anne's interest is absorbed with innocent flirtation and the excitement of having a particular boyfriend, as distinct from the passing attentions of various boys in her class, whom she speaks of with good-humoured condescension. She obviously enjoys the memory of her adroit techniques for handling their overenthusiastic advances (p. 16). Although very pleased to have the handsome Harry as a boyfriend, Anne knows her mind and is firmly in control of the situation. She recognizes she is 'not in love' and is flattered, in a casual way, by the fact that Harry's feelings for her are much more ardent than hers. While enjoying his company, she is delighted when the admired Peter Wessel greets her in the street. She is becoming interested in boys and knows that she is attractive to them, but is far too sensible to allow herself to imagine that she wants much more than friendship. (It is however worth noting the underlying strength of her feeling for Peter Wessel, seen in some detail in the early letters of 1944 when her relationship with Peter Van Daan intensifies into romantic love.)

This single-minded self-control is also apparent in Anne's attitude to school. While obviously a lively, popular and independent pupil, she has a clear vision of the importance of work and study, developed later in her very clear ambition to become a writer and to rise above the mundane example of feminine achievement represented by the women around her (see pp. 194 and 212).

Her originality is amusingly illustrated by the way she responds to the essays set by her teacher, Mr Keptor, as punishments for talking. She combines ingenuity, humour and charm in responses which leave the teacher willingly defeated; there is no malice or grudging compliance in her attitude, but rather a positive, vigorous meeting of a situation head on to make the best of it. This quality of optimism, of relishing a challenge, is characteristic of Anne's writing throughout the *Diary* and is evident in her refusal to submit to the pressures of life in the annexe.

A more reflective and sober side of her nature is seen in the entry of 20 June. Again, we see the beginnings of a theme that is echoed throughout the book; here it is Anne's sense of spiritual isolation while surrounded by lively company. Though in no way introverted, she is clearly aware that mere friendship and family bonds do not automatically create opportunities for the deeper matters which she feels the need to share. The diary was an inspired choice of birthday present for Anne in that it gave her exactly the right opportunity to address these profound feelings without fear of misunderstanding or criticism. She knows that she has thoughts and feelings which need serious examination and finds in the diary a means of focusing on them in a controlled, objective way. Note her natural, conversational style – 'Let me put it more clearly . . .' (p. 14), which indicates a balanced, rational approach to her subject matter, an approach which rejects the temptation towards maudlin indulgence or fruitless speculation. She is too positive for such pointless rambling and sees her writing very much as a process of self-discovery which it is her duty to conduct as honestly and usefully as she can.

The second half of the entry details briefly the preliminary anti-Semitic tactics used by the Nazis to harass and control the Dutch Jewish population. The repetitive listing of the restrictions not only conveys a sense of the formalized oppression to which all Jews were exposed, but is also the voice of a helpless victim employing the natural rhetoric of indignation against unreasonable punishment.

Glossary Section 1

p. 13 **Rin-Tin-Tin** A famous dog who starred in children's adventure films.

p. 15 **Pogroms** Anti-Semitic massacres in Germany. The most notorious was the Kristallnacht (Crystal Night) of 10 November 1938 in which Jewish premises in Berlin were looted and burned, and Jews beaten and imprisoned by the Nazis.

p. 16 **'masis'** A misprint for the 'Oasis' ice-cream shop.

p. 20 **Zionist Movement** A Jewish organization which aimed to make Palestine the official home of the Jewish nation.

p. 21 **'dangerous for Jews to be out after eight o'clock'** The evening curfew mentioned in the entry of 20 June. Breaking curfew could lead to punishment.

p. 21 *vix satis* Latin for 'just enough', i.e. a barely acceptable grade.

p. 22 *cum laude* Latin for 'with honours' – a distinction.

Section 2 8 July 1942 – 21 August 1942

In the last entry for Sunday 5 July, Anne remembered a recent conversation with her father in which he had broached the subject of going into hiding, as many Jews had already done. She concluded with a passionate plea for a stay of execution, a plea which was ironically rejected later that day as the Germans sent a call-up notice for Margot that afternoon. This second section deals with the Franks' response to the call-up, the process of moving and settling into the *achterhuis* above 263 Prinsengracht, and the arrival of the Van Daans.

Anne's record of how the bad news was received is sombre, but unexaggerated and demonstrates clearly her gift of fresh, unforced description and vivid creation of atmosphere. She has a sure sense of the dramatic while never falling into the trap of being melodramatic. For example, on page 23 she evokes the tension as she and Margot wait alone at home for their parents. Notice how the narrative shifts in tense 'It was a great shock . . . should we allow him to be doomed' and is then interrupted with one word – 'silence', breaking abruptly into the rhythm of the sentences and conveying perfectly the numbing effect of the news. See how they 'creep softly' rather than go quietly to answer the door. The tension is alive, permanently caught in the specific vocabulary of fear and concealment. The narrative then collapses into a semi-coherent string of questions as she speculates fearfully about what they will do, not knowing that her father had already made contingency plans against the day when they would need to escape German persecution by hiding permanently in a secret home.

The interest of this section lies in Anne's ability to depict her feelings and to describe forcefully and evocatively the despair she and Margot experienced. We could be reading fiction, in which it is relatively easy to invent situations and moods. What is far more difficult is the balanced recreation of inner states of emotional reaction in a form that is accessible and plausible to a reader distanced by personal safety and several decades from the events she describes.

As Anne moves away from the early moments of terror and uncertainty, she becomes caught up in recording the welter of practical activities needed to accomplish the move safely and unobtrusively. There is even time for a touch of humour in her complaint about the discomfort caused by wearing layers of clothes, necessitated by the fact that they dare not carry suit-cases. Her linguistic facility, evident in the natural use of simile ('as if we were going to the North Pole') and her clear cogent organization of her material is apparent even in the account of the inside of the warehouse and the rooms above. Everything is observed economically and yet with a sure sense of audience that demands more than just factual information. On page 26 for example, she adopts the premises which become 'our' home and she gleefully rejoices in the secrecy of their Annexe. It reads like a guided tour – 'a little step . . . and then you are inside.' She has a child's capacity to be fascinated by a new situation, evident in the enthusiasm with which she shows us around. Her vivid portrayal of the dirt and disorder which greeted them carries the same mark of the compulsive writer – note the use of *hyperbole* as she relates how the rooms were 'chock full' of rubbish, the little bedroom 'filled to the ceiling' with clothes and bedding, her mother and Margot 'not fit to move a muscle'.

She soon becomes proud of their new home and, again hyperbolically, issues a challenge to find a better sanctuary anywhere in the country. The details of domestic adaptation however merge quickly into an awareness that this is a last chance of escape and that any mistakes, such as coughing loudly, may lead to discovery. The nature of their situation is encapsulated perfectly in her emphatic recognition that they are to all intents and purposes prisoners, 'never' allowed out of the building (p. 29). Close study of the description and diagram of the building (pp. 25–7) gives a very clear indication of just how cramped the accommodation was. The eight refugees were crammed into the two smaller blocks shown in the upper halves of the second and third floors in the diagram. They shared one toilet and washbasin which were situated in a small room, one door of which led directly to Anne's and Margot's study/bedroom. The Van Daans' bedroom on the third floor was also the kitchen and general living room for the whole group.

Her natural optimism reasserts itself with the arrival of the Van Daans and we are reminded of the high standards she expects from her companions as she labels their son Peter a 'gawky youth' (p. 30). She had from her own account been popular at school, notable for her irrepressible high spirits and sense of fun. Her briskly dismissive tone of voice is not scornful or hostile, but reveals her frustration and disappointment as she knows the coming isolation will be bearable only if the Annexe is filled with a sense of fun and camaraderie. Her exasperation at Peter's indolence (apparent on p. 31), reinforces our growing understanding of an active, quick-witted girl, for whom enforced inactivity is going to be fretting and irksome experience.

A family friend, Miep Van Senten, has written about Anne and comments on her talent for mimicry. See how this is indicated in the fluid, easy prose of her account of Mr Van Daan's harmless deception of the Franks' lodger about their whereabouts. Clearly, this is not a verbatim account, although the use of the first person enhances the credibility of the report through the sense of immediacy it creates. At this stage we become not just Anne Frank's readers, but also part of Mr Van Daan's audience as he talks directly to the people in front of him. Compare for example the spontaneous natural diction of '"Mr Goudsmit"— I said— "it suddenly dawns on me. . ."' with the flat reportage of a possible alternative which would carry the same factual information. For example, 'Mr Van Daan told us *that* he had spoken to Mr Goudsmit' and so on. This contrast forms the basis of the assignment at the end of this section.

What characterizes and enlivens Anne's rendition of Van Daan's story is her ability to step into his shoes and retell the story, not necessarily in his language (although I think she captures well the slightly pompous quality of some adults' speech), but with a wealth of incidental detail and a sense of timing appropriate to a spoken rather than a written situation. Similarly, she is not content just to mention Mrs Van Daan's eccentric arrival with her chamberpot, but imbues it with real humour by the use of direct speech, the use of 'declared', the formality of which contrasts superbly with the ludicrous picture Mrs Van Daan presents, and the accompanying picture of Mr Van Daan standing somewhat ineffectually with a tea towel under his arm (p. 30). It is this capacity for mimicry that makes her dialogue convincing; she *hears* conversations as she partly remembers them. At thirteen, she already knows that for her the life of the mind is more important than ordinary, more mundane occupations. Consider the random list of belongings she snatches together as they prepare to leave their home; old letters are preferred to dresses for the sake of the memories she values so highly. Her writing is in itself clear evidence of her need to create something lasting and meaningful from a situation which many people, young or old, would have found devoid of hope or interest.

Glossary Section 2

p. 22 **SS** Schutzstaffel (Elite Nazi Party unit: provided Hitler's bodyguard, combat units, and later concentration camp guards).

p. 22 **call-up notice** Written notification of conscription, apparently for forced labour in Germany, but in reality often a prelude to torture or death.

p. 24 **We let our large upstairs room** A common practice in Amsterdam in the 1930s and 1940s as the city was full of religious and political refugees. Over-population even led to lodgers taking in lodgers. (See *Anne Frank Remembered* by Miep Gies, p. 34.)

p. 25 *via* By way of.

p. 27 **Prinsengracht** A canal street in old Amsterdam, bordering the Jordaan district. The street was full of small businesses and warehouses and therefore the possibilities of discovery were lessened as the neighbouring buildings would have been unoccupied after business hours.

p. 28 **Westertoren clock** Part of the Westerkerk tower which is close to the building and can be seen from the office window.

p. 30 **Maastricht** Dutch city on the German/Belgian border, on the route for anyone escaping from Amsterdam to Switzerland. A piece of quick thinking on the part of Mr Van Daan.

Assignments Sections 1 and 2

1 You will find it helpful to make a list of the characters and their relationship to Anne. Several names are mentioned and can lead to confusion, particularly because they are not English. Virtually all the people in the book are named in the first two sections (pages 13–31).

2 Try keeping a diary for a week or two. Do not feel bound to make daily entries, but concentrate on observing people and try to organize your material coherently. Avoid the temptation to dwell on your own feelings unless you have a particular reason for doing so. This is a long assignment, perhaps over a thousand words.

3 Write an account of a real conversation – aim for a fresh, lively style rather than mere accuracy. Perhaps two hundred words.

4 Try writing Anne's account of Mr Van Daan's story on page 26. Use the third person (e.g. 'Mr Van Daan said that . . .') stick to the facts and leave out what could be seen as unnecessary non-factual material. Make a note of what you omit, find a way of describing it and then think and write about how this added element enhances the quality of Anne's writing. Are the *facts* actually as interesting as the *way* she presents them?

Section 3 2 September 1942–16 October 1942

The last section ended with a hint of the domestic tension inevitable in such a claustrophobic situation. This is now amplified in much detail, with eloquent accounts of the nature of the friction that developed both within and between the two families.

Although Anne is never bitter, it is quite clear that she sees one person as being particularly responsible for the scenes and awkward atmospheres amongst the group. Mrs Van Daan is exposed as a silly, lazy, moody and hypocritical woman whose pretentiousness stems from a shallow, selfish nature.

As the youngest member of the refugees, Anne is an easy target for Mrs Van Daan's hollow lectures on good behaviour. When relating these incidents, Anne is never content simply to describe a situation in indirect speech. Instead she enlivens her narrative with direct appeals to the imaginary 'Kitty' and appears to revel in repeating or, to some extent, in inventing snatches of conversation. These never fail to transform an already lively account into a vivid and often amusing scene. Notice how on p. 32 she captures the cadences both of annoyance and habitual nagging in Mrs Van Daan's voice as she shouts at Anne for breaking one of her soup plates. The extra touch of 'for once' economically and deftly defines the attitude of someone who will seize an opportunity to scold rather than just react in anger. The spoken words, brief as they are, are absolutely necessary for an artistically true portrayal of the domestic drama that the group enacts. Drama is not too strong a term, for it is important to remember the international situation that forced them, and thousands like them, to exile within their own country. Naturally enough the permanent undercurrent of tension caused by the constant need to preserve silence and secrecy and the rareness of privacy provoked emotional tantrums that would have been unlikely in more normal circumstances.

Mr Van Daan's exaggerated response when dealing with Peter's rebellion on p. 33 gives a clear example of a sudden outburst of unnecessarily vehement anger. The situation is not extreme – a mild case of adolescent misbehaviour – but the father's latent anxiety, compounded by the embarrassment inevitable in a public confrontation, leads to an ugly scene which

Otto Frank, Anne's father, has to resolve.

The impact of this event on Anne is obviously significant. She finds angry demonstrations a novel experience, and she comments at the beginning of the section about how unmannerly the Van Daans' behaviour towards each other is when compared to that of her own parents.

Although Anne's father and Mr Van Daan had been business colleagues, the two families are obviously very different. The Franks' habits of work, study, reading and civilized discussion contrast strongly with the less reasonable, more selfish, materialistic practices of the Van Daans. (The entry for 6 July 1944 shows just how accurately Ann came to understand this cultural distinction.) Anne makes a number of references to her own reading, both in English and in Dutch, and has ambitious academic plans. Her sister Margot and her mother also value study and reading, while in contrast Peter Van Daan 'sighs and groans' over his work (p. 34).

Anne's intelligence appears to antagonize Mrs Van Daan, whose infuriating injunctions about behaviour and courtesy merely provoke Anne into making 'cheeky answers'. Her parents support her in her refusal to be bullied and take it upon themselves to reproach Mrs Van Daan by exposing the fallacies in her statements. It is interesting to note that there is no mention of her husband coming to her defence; perhaps like Anne he enjoyed seeing her arguments used against her to good effect! See for example the conversations about vegetables (p. 37) and modesty (p. 39).

Anne's gift for writing is not restricted to the portrayal of acrimonious scenes; her enthusiasm for humorous description is evident in her account of the primitive bathing arrangements and in that of the improvised lavatory facilities compelled by the plumber's visit (p. 40). Her ability to see the funny side of the situation and her refusal to indulge in self-pity, especially as this was originally a private diary, is unusual. While she is never falsely optimistic, she seems determined to make the most of their predicament and never to succumb to its pressures for any longer than she can help.

The grim realities of Nazi occupation and anti-Semitism take up the whole of one entry (9 October). Anne touches quickly and surely on a number of different issues. She describes graphically the appalling conditions in concentration camps, the indiscriminate call-ups which made no allowance for age or sex, the dangers of Allied air attacks and the murder of hostages as reprisal against sabotage, presumably by Dutch resistance operators. But even when describing these atrocities, her style never becomes journalistic. Her comments are always informed by an intense personal response: 'I feel terribly upset'; 'the poor old thing'. At these points, her authorial voice becomes passionate. For her, 'Kitty' is real and we read not so much a diary entry as one half of a conversation. Note the questions and the repeated use of 'you', which reveals the extent of her imaginative involvement in her writing.

The spontaneous informality of her approach signified by the questions, exclamations and shifts from the third to the first person, achieves an authenticity and sincerity of purpose denied to less talented diarists. She homes in instinctively on matters of interest, whether personal or international, and allows her response to each situation to shape her commentary about it. Because of this natural, fresh approach to her subject matter, it is easy to overlook the signs of thoughtfulness and insight that are another main attribute of Anne's diary. Although she is barely thirteen, she sees very clearly into the motives and fallacies that lie behind what people say and do. She does not become a ruthless critic of those around her, however, but understands, for example, that it is Peter's 'curiosity' which prompts his disobedience over reading a book his father had prohibited (p. 33).

Note too the clear organization of the account she gives of the arrangements made by the men to maintain contact with their firm's representative (p. 36). The sentence structure is logically sequenced and explains very simply and effectively the procedures and reasons for such action.

This section already shows some signs of literary development when compared to the first two. The scope of Anne's material has increased and she provides in response a considerable variety of styles, moods and subjects. There is clear evidence of humour, anger, compassion, understanding and an uncommonly developed literary ability whose promise is more than fulfilled as we read on.

Glossary Section 3

p. 33 **then everyone was in the private office listening to the radio** Probably listening to a BBC broadcast – a punishable offence, but a valuable morale booster.

p. 35 **Prince Bernhard, Princess Juliana** Son-in-law and daughter of Queen Wilhemina of the Netherlands. The Dutch Royal Family escaped to England when Germany invaded Holland.

p. 36 **Zeeland** Area to the south of Holland, bordering Belgium.

p. 37 **Mevrouw** Reference to Mrs Van Daan, slightly unflattering in that it suggests she was not a Juffrouw (genteel woman).

p. 39 **fishwife** Another unflattering term. Anne clearly felt Mrs Van Daan was unladylike.

p. 41 **'Miss Quack-Quack'** See *Diary*, 21 June 1942.

p. 43 **distant and barbarous regions** Possibly a reference to the infamous Nazi concentration camps at Dachau in Germany and Auschwitz in Poland.

p. 43 **Gestapo** Geheime Staatspolizei, the Nazi secret police, operating in all the occupied territories; responsible for the suppression of subversion and underground activity.

Section 4 20 October 1942–13 January 1943

The growing ease with which Anne writes is the first thing we notice as we examine this section. The entries are becoming longer and there is a new note of maturity in the recognition that all the two families can do is to wait and pray for an Allied victory. There is still plenty of gossip about her feelings and mundane day to day events, but the horizons of her interests and understanding have extended as her ability to recreate scenes and to discuss important issues steadily develops.

The first and last entries concentrate mainly on the war, and are added to by passing references to it in interim letters. The first reference (20 October) is purely about the group and is concerned with a particular event which frightened them all. It reminds us of just how flimsy their protection was from capture by the Nazis, partly because of the very nature of the event itself, but also by the sense of tension Anne evokes as the carpenter (p. 45) inadvertently alarms them by working immediately outside the secret entrance to their hideout. (See the entry for 21 August 1942 for details of the hidden entrance.) As with her description of their feelings when Margot's call-up notice from the SS arrived (8 July 1942), the atmosphere is edgy, evident in the details of her shaking hand, their pale faces and how she 'nearly fainted'. Again it is her natural sense of audience, an inner ear for a good tale, which forges the information together into an episode which grabs our attention. We could be reading a scene from a thriller – the same elements are there. And yet, behind this vivid account of near discovery, lies a very childlike and primitive expression of her fear; she imagines the intruder to be a combination of a giant and a Fascist. The incongruity of the two terms would be laughable but for two things. Firstly, the appalling danger they were in forbids any element of humour, and secondly, we are forced to remember that we are reading the work of a young girl whose unusual powers of writing ultimately have to make way for the elemental childhood language of fairy-tales when she is faced with serious danger.

Brief, general comments about the war crop up throughout this section, pithy summaries which show her awareness of the situation. She understands clearly, for example, Winston Churchill's cautious agreement with the popular optimism following British forces' success in establishing military footholds (9 November 1942). On 19 November she writes with real pathos of the ongoing plight of the Jews in Amsterdam. The heavy, measured pace and alliteration (words beginning with the same letters) of 'Evening after evening the green and grey army lorries trundle past' (p. 54) reminds us of the sombre rhythms of the First World War poetry of Siegfried Sassoon and Wilfred Owen. (Read the opening stanza of Owen's 'Dulce et decorum est'.) The mood is subdued, the vocabulary direct and challenging.

This tone, a blend of anger, compassion and a reluctant gratitude for her own safety, is echoed more forcefully on 13 January 1943 when she catalogues the misery endured by so many of her people. The relentless nature of the Jews' suffering is emphasized in the frequent references to quantity in this entry. It is as if Anne is overwhelmed by the enormous scale of events and has to express some kind of corresponding response – 'hundreds and thousands of people ... whole globe ... millions ... countless'. It is an impassioned statement, shot through with a fierce natural expression fuelled by a complex set of emotions – 'no coat, no hat, no stockings, and no one helps ...' (p. 63). Her feelings of horror and helplessness are however not allowed to dominate her thoughts. With a very practical wisdom she knows that it is impossible and undesirable to sustain a morbid attitude and she enthusiastically records Mr Van Daan's spoof guide to their annexe (17 November 1942). It is a mark of her fundamental good spirits that she is able to view the deprivations of the hideout with humour and we remember the lively, popular, carefree girl we met in the opening pages of the diary.

Less urgent, but important issues can be seen in the fragmented entry of 20 October. Six paragraphs each deal with a separate subject, each of which indicates to some extent either the difficult nature of their situation (it is impossible to call a doctor to Otto Frank when he falls ill) or aspects of Anne's own attitudes. We learn that she is fast approaching puberty as she eagerly expects menstruation to start, and with this reminder of her age, we are surprised to read that she is going to read Goethe and Schiller with her father. As we think again of the Franks' cultured background, we might be tempted to contrast her wide tastes in reading with much of the literary diet that is currently offered to young people via so-called teenage fiction. Evidence of Anne's own sound literary judgement can be seen in her comment about the apparently more adult book she has been reading (p. 46), correctly identifying it as little more than a schoolgirl love story. It was presumably discarded in favour of more interesting and satisfying material.

It is reasonable to assume that Anne's fondness for challenging books contributed to her own writing talents and to her ability to read beneath the superficial aspects of her relationships with others. The letter of 7 November 1942 is remarkable not only for its fluency and clarity, but for the maturity of Anne's perception of herself and her family. She carefully examines how she feels about them, candidly and without self-pity, and demonstrates an uncommon capacity for objective analysis, seeing very clearly the nature of her feelings for her parents. Her criticism of her mother and her worship of her father are acutely investigated, as are her own attitudes and failings. This is no conventional uprush of rebellion; it derives from the action of an honest conscience founded on a sincere religious faith and 'Kitty' takes on the confidential status of a trusted friend, who will listen and help. There is no doubt that for Anne her diary was a means of controlling and coping with the pressures of life in the annexe. It allowed her to achieve a balanced response to her own feelings and became an intellectual resource which developed her considerable natural talent. Although this particular entry addresses the difficult issue of favouritism in a family, Anne never allows herself to degenerate into sullen self-pity or to exaggerate her sense of grievance. Her love for her family and her intelligent awareness of the limits of other people's abilities are condensed into the recognition that it is impossible for parents to 'succeed in making their children absolutely content' (p. 48). Caught between childhood and adulthood, she is faced with the difficult task of admitting that her parents are fallible and that even her adored father 'cannot take the place of my entire little world of bygone days' (p. 56). It is to her credit that she can feel angry while maintaining affection for her parents. Similarly, her acceptance of Margot's cleverness and beauty is untainted by jealousy, for her search for self-understanding is too sincere to be hindered by bitterness or petty competition.

We see her generosity in a very different context as she relates the arrival of the eighth and final member of the group of Jewish refugees (17 and 19 November 1942). Although she admits she does not really enjoy sharing her possessions with a stranger (p. 54), she recognizes that Albert Dussel's need is identical to that of the others and rejoices in their corporate safety. Even when he turns out to be less pleasant company than she had imagined (28 November 1942), she refuses to dwell on his failings and winds up the day's entry in a whirl of amused contradiction.

Anne's love of fun ripples throughout the diary. There is a wonderful portrayal of the chaos caused by Mr Van Daan's sausage making (10 December 1942), reminiscent of the vivid scenes of disorder in Dickens' *Pickwick Papers*. Anne's memory for detail and her sure instinct for material which will enliven her diary is very good here and also when relating the incident of the spilt beans (9 November 1942). It is even better however when, with some justification, she gleefully describes Mrs Van Daan's suffering as she is treated for toothache by Dussel, a qualified dentist. The scene is riotous and clearly caused much amusement to all the spectators, especially Anne. There is no malice in her account and she freely admits that she would have made an even bigger fuss. Given her resentment at Mrs Van Daan's persistent nagging, Anne's refusal to scorn her enemy suggests that her wish to 'improve myself' (p. 49) is no empty resolution.

The section ends on a sombre note similar to that of 19 November 1942. The closing words of the entry for 13 January 1943 are notable for the grave repetition of 'wait', a process that will lead either to liberation or death. The irony and pathos arising from our knowledge of Anne's death just over two years later intertwine to form a tragic prophecy that is both moving and condemnatory of the power that murdered her and some six million of her fellow Jews.

Glossary Section 4

p. 45 **bookcase door** See entry for Friday 21 August 1942 and map on p. 26 of the diary.

p. 45 **Elli** Elli Vossen. A typist at Travies & Co., trusted by the refugees.

p. 45 **Miep** Miep Van Senten. Another friend, Travies' colleague and contact with the outside world. See pages 23 and 24.

p. 45 **Fascist** Technically, a member of the extreme right-wing political party which ruled Italy from 1922 to 1943. Used here in a more general sense to refer to Hitler's Nazi forces.

p. 46 **furniture . . . removed** i.e. by German authorities following their failure to arrest the Van Daans.

p. 46 **Goethe and Schiller** Eighteenth and early nineteenth-century German writers, mainly of drama and poetry.

p. 46 **Don Carlos** Blank verse drama by Schiller.

p. 49 **greedy pigs** i.e. the Van Daans.

p. 52 **yellow star** See entry for 20 June 1942, p. 15.

p. 57 **St. Nicholas Day** Dutch festival in early December mainly for children.

p. 58 **Black Peter** Legendary Dutch figure associated with St Nicholas.

p. 59 **Pim** Anne's nickname for her father.

p. 62 **hundreds of 'planes** Belonging to the Allied forces.

Assignments Sections 3 and 4

1 The refugees could not go out, had only limited contact with free people, could only use the radio at certain safe times and of course had no television. Make a detailed programme of a week's activities for any one of them (apart from Anne). Include domestic activities (eating, washing, etc), household chores, entertainment, study, exercise and anything else you can think of. Be as inventive as possible and make the programme suit the person.

2 Assignment no. 2 (Sections 1 and 2) asked you to keep a diary.

Now include some entries which refer to events you have read of in the newspapers and which affect you. News about teacher shortage and textbook provision might be particularly relevant to you.

3 As a development of assignment no. 3 (Sections 1 and 2), write a conversation between Otto and Edith Frank in which they discuss their situation. Refer to safety, their children, domestic issues, the past, the future, war news and other likely subjects. Aim at about four hundred words.

4 (A difficult assignment which you may find requires too personal a response for your liking.) Examine your attitudes to your parents. Be honest about your feelings, and use incidents which have stuck in your mind. It is also important to think how fair your comments are.

5 Although this is a literary guide, some historical research will be very useful for a fuller understanding of the diary. Two main areas are relevant: Holland under German occupation and the Holocaust (the Nazis' attempt to rid Europe of the Jews). Do some preliminary reading using the bibliography at the end of this book. A useful starting point will be to establish the main facts of the German invasion of Holland in 1940.

Section 5 30 January 1943–19 July 1943

Anne's uncertain and at times turbulent feelings about the rest of her family are very much to the fore in this section. There is open anger and frustration, supported by a more serious awareness of the distance that lies between her and her mother. The first entry is very revealing. It fluently describes the resentment and pain she feels at what she sees as constant criticism from the others – the simile 'like shafts from a tightly strung bow' (p. 63) is pithy and appropriate – but there is also considerable dignity and maturity in her decision to conceal her hurt. She knows that an outburst would elicit sympathy and overt attempts by the others to be pleasant to her, but she correctly sees that such a situation would leave her emotionally and psychologically indebted to them. Her desire for independence is too precious to accept such an unsatisfactory state of affairs and so she assumes a brave face to conceal her unhappiness.

The extent of her misery is forcefully conveyed in the battery of complaints on p. 63. The repetition of 'if I . . .' applied to completely opposing aspects of her behaviour emphasizes the impossibility, in her eyes, of ever reaching a satisfactory state of relations with the others. She is of course not being singled out for special attention. The daily dangers and difficulties of living in the annexe are a constant source of friction for the group, to the extent that rows are commonplace and seen as inevitable (5 February 1943, 27 April 1943). Of the three young people, however, Anne was clearly the liveliest and therefore had the most potential to draw attention to herself. (See her comments about Peter and Margot, 5 February 1943.) She returns to the subject of the constant lectures she endures (11 July 1943) and reveals that she has learnt one method of coping. She has become aware that her habit of unrestrained comment can be irritating and reluctantly concedes that silence is a better policy.

These two aspects of concealment – pretending to be cheerful and keeping quiet – mark a turn in her understanding of herself. She sees into how people are likely to behave in a given situation and, equally importantly, she begins to see how others view her behaviour. This level of self-awareness shows that she is quickly outgrowing childhood and that she is willing to carry out what must have been some very difficult exercises in self-control.

Another example of her dawning adolescence is her clear-sighted view of the need to accept the emotional chasm between her and her mother. Although there is some similarity between this and her understanding that her father can no longer be the centre of her life (section 4), the impetus behind each decision comes from a very different direction. In her father's case, Anne came to see that he had faults like everyone else. This new understanding is made very clear in the poignant picture she presents of Otto Frank caught in a moment of discomfort or illness: 'He looked exactly like some shrivelled-up old man from an old people's home' (p. 59). But when speaking of her mother, Anne recognizes that the time has come to abandon any hypocritical pretence of closeness between them. The letter of 2 April 1943 in which Anne recounts her rejection of her mother's company to bed-time prayers is notable for its controlled treatment of an upsetting situation. There is no self-pity, no facile clichéd nonsense about a 'generation gap'. It is simply a dispassionate analysis of the upsetting truth, that for a variety of reasons, Anne and her mother had reached a parting of the ways.

It is an astonishing scene. Everything is quiet and unexaggerated, with a marked absence of any hostility towards her mother. It has been said before that 'Kitty' acted to some extent as a trusted friend and the tone of this entry suggests a conversation between two people who are close enough to share a serious problem. There is no element of malicious gossip or of a desire on Anne's part to elevate herself above her mother, but rather a quietly urgent need to express and examine the situation. No appeal for sympathy is made to a reader, real or imaginary, and there is no self-pity. Everything is precise, balanced (in contrast perhaps to some of her complaints about less important problems) and fair-minded. Had she lived, Anne might have looked back on this and seen that such a punctilious approach in itself indicated a deeper love for her mother than she was aware of at the time. Similarly, her concern to avoid condemning her mother is very apparent in the description of her disappointment, the 'distorted look on her face' and the 'tears in her eyes' (p. 73). At the same time however, Anne knows that she must not conceal her real feelings. She refers openly but succinctly to her mother's failings before passing on to an appraisal of her own new attitude. The whole passage is immensely clear-sighted and controlled. It is remarkable both for the youth of its writer and for the delicate precision with which Anne treats her subject. She writes reluctantly, but with a courage and honesty which characterizes so much of her diary.

Despite this underlying source of unhappiness, there is much amusement and vivacity throughout the section. Humour would have been an essential way of easing the tensions of life in the annexe, and Anne captures the invigorating quality of events which allowed them, however briefly, to behave like free people and laugh unrestrainedly at a ludicrous situation or individual errors. Peter Van Daan's imperfect understanding of French and the consequently indelicate nature of his notice is a delightful example of such a situation.

It may be coincidence that causes Mrs Van Daan to be selected for special attention in Anne's diary when amusing stories are told. On the other hand however, knowing the frequent friction between them and Anne's scant respect for Mrs Van Daan, it is not unreasonable to suspect that Anne enjoyed recording her rival's discomfort, particularly when it arose from her own silliness. Two incidents stand out as clear examples of Mrs Van Daan's tendency to say or do the wrong thing. In the entry for 5 February 1943, her ridiculous anecdote about her own flirtatiousness and her father's advice about how to handle overenthusiastic advances from men unintentionally provokes a hilarious response. Notice how Anne draws attention to Mrs Van Daan's total lack of awareness of the 'perfect nonsense' she was spouting: the use of 'and do you know' implies strongly that the story is meant to impress her audience, and the humour therefore derives from the contrast between the speaker's intention and the actual nature and reception of what she said.

Another shining example of Mrs Van Daan's considerable talent for inept and inappropriate behaviour lies at the end of the entry for 18 May 1943. As the Van Daans' room was at the very top of the warehouse, they were most vulnerable in the event of bombing. Given this danger, it was excusable for Mrs Van Daan to run downstairs, but definitely unwise for her to seek shelter in Albert Dussel's room. He was clearly not a man to shy away from a humorous suggestion of impropriety ('Come into my bed'), which would have further diminished her impoverished stock of dignity and authority over Anne, who shared a room with Dussel.

As always, the quality of Anne's presentation of these and other scenes is enriched by her clear enjoyment of describing fully, but always relevantly, events which were in one way or another worthy of recording. This description is enhanced by snippets of dialogue which underline and consolidate her portrayal of a particular person. Anne's sure instinct for just the right sample of someone's speech has the great merit of allowing the subjects of Anne's attention to speak for themselves. The result is that the effect is natural and buoyant, with a complete absence of any contrived conversation. She also imbues these incidents with the quality of a more consistent narrative by using quoted speech as the climax to a passage of description or commentary about a person. This means that, although she may include several unrelated incidents in one entry, there is a sense of coherence and continuity arising from the reader having received Anne's own impressions of what was important and interesting for that day: see for example how she simultaneously records and exposes, for the propagandist nonsense they were,

Hitler's radio interviews with wounded German soldiers (p. 69). By isolating the essential exchange of words, the puerile and heartless quality of the intention behind the programme – to publicize the claimed heroism of the German army via a broadcast display of maimed men – is highlighted and condemned.

Other war news focuses on two main areas: reports of the effects of combat and Dutch resistance activity (27 April 1943), and the increasing difficulties faced by the Dutch citizens as the Germans tighten their hold on the country. This is exemplified in the decree that all students, who would in their adult lives be in responsible and therefore potentially influential positions, should indicate support for the Nazi regime – 18 May 1943. The second area can itself be seen from two angles: the general extent of privation and suffering experienced by the Dutch and the particular problems faced by the residents of the *achterhuis*.

The bombing of Amsterdam by Allied forces in an attempt to demolish key German strongholds inevitably had tragic consequences for many Dutch people (19 July 1943). Although some humour had to be wrenched from the appalling situation (18 May 1943), the German occupation brought a twofold danger for the Dutch and added to the anxiety and hardship of the Franks, Van Daans and Dussel.

The entries for 27 April and 1 May 1943 bluntly state the reality of life in the annexe and go a long way towards explaining the rows Anne frequently refers to. In the light of this information, her comments about the Van Daans' greed over a little margarine (27 February 1943) appear less petulant, and her support for her mother (12 March 1943) less exaggerated than we might have supposed. Keeping one's morale high when faced by cramped conditions, hunger, dirt and uncomfortable, ill-fitting clothes is hard. Doing so while constantly keeping alert against the possibility of discovery in a damp, rat-infested building (10 March 1943) was at times an intolerable strain which must have provoked many scenes such as the one between Anne and Dussel over the issue of shared use of the table in their room (13 July 1943).

The privations, dangers and tensions of life in the annexe occupy a good deal of this section. Anne is clearly dependent on her own creative resources and spends much time trying to work out how best to find her own place in the mix of ages and personalities in the hideout. No startling change has occurred in the nature of her diary, but there is a sense of the strain of settling into such a compromised and difficult way of life.

Glossary Section 5

p. 64 **The golden mean** i.e. tread a middle path between the extremes of very good or very bad behaviour.

p. 65 **S.V.P.** S'il vous plait – French for 'if you please'.

p. 65 **Gandhi of India** Mahatma Gandhi. Indian leader committed to non-violence.

p. 65 **A.A. guns** Anti-aircraft guns.

p. 69 **"Führer aller Germanen"** Hitler, speaking on the official radio broadcast of German music and propaganda.

p. 71 **Westertoren** See the glossary for section 2 or p. 28 of the diary (11 July 1942).

p. 75 **oilcloth** Cheap functional unattractive table covering.

p. 76 **All students . . . New Order** See also *Corrie ten Boom: Her Life, Her Faith* p. 81.

p. 78 **hand in our radio** The Germans called in radios to prevent the Dutch listening to anti-German news from England. "Our radio" would refer to the set owned by Travies & Co. in the offices beneath the hideout.

Section 6 23 July 1943–11 November 1943

The dominant impression in this section is of Anne's wish to portray in detail a comprehensive range of day-to-day events and situations that made up the refugees' life in the annexe. Although this is of course to some extent true of the diary as a whole, there is greater attention paid here to describing the various routines that were necessary to coexistence in their cramped and insecure premises. News about the war is correspondingly diminished, although the entry for 10 September reflects strongly the joy felt by all nations opposed to fascism at the news that Italy, Germany's ally, had surrendered to Allied forces.

The concern with daily habits and incidents reflects and partly explains the consistency of the frequent disagreements and open rows that flared up in the annexe. In such a claustrophobic situation one's attention would inevitably be forced towards the most trivial matters, and minor differences of opinion would be amplified into major issues of principle. The entry for 29 July

1943 shows this very clearly, and is presented through Anne's customary technique of turning narrative into dialogue, so that the characterization of the people involved gains in dramatic stature and Anne stands on the dividing line between author and diarist. Her expression of a minor reservation about *Henry from the Other Side* provoked an intolerant tirade of disparagement from Mr Dussel who, abetted by Mrs Van Daan, seized the opportunity to berate Anne about her lack of experience, her precocity and what they felt was her poor upbringing.

Given their groundless hostility, Anne's practice of relating a very passable imitation of their comments has the effect of allowing them to be condemned out of their own mouths. It is unlikely that we would find Dussel's overbearing pomposity and Mrs Van Daan's general silliness so convincing if we had heard about them in Anne's words alone. She has the gift of capturing the essential nature or flavour of a person's speech, and therefore provides a transparent medium by which we are allowed to experience for ourselves the quality of life above the warehouse.

To complement the effect of directly seeing the adults' unjust accusations of her, we also sense Anne's fury in her frequent exclamations and open hostility, particularly directed towards Mrs Van Daan. The final paragraph of the entry boils over with bitter and potentially libellous recriminations against Mrs Van Daan, compressed into a catalogue of pungent condemnation. In view of what we know of her, it is unlikely that she completely merits such an attack, and Anne herself acknowledges the imprudent excesses that her anger temporarily caused.

Irritating as it was, this particular situation at least sparks off some energy and, eventually, a wry concession that reveals Anne's fundamental good nature and sense of humour. More seriously upsetting for her was the pervasive atmosphere of bad feeling that had clearly developed for a number of reasons. The long-standing tension resulting from the forced intimacy and secrecy of their existence naturally acted as a fertile soil for more temporary problems, two of which are revealed in the entry for 16 September 1943. The imminent harsh Dutch winter would have caused great concern to the refugees as they depended on Miep Van Senten, an employee of Travies & Co., to provide their food and other essential items, and the worsening weather would have made her task much harder. To shop secretly for eight extra people was an enormous strain for her at any time.

To do so in heavy rain or snow when less food was available in the shops was to impose a dangerously heavy burden, for her frequent and lengthy shopping trips would sooner or later cause suspicion to be thrown on her, and could lead to the discovery of the annexe by the authorities.

Other worrying factors were the problem of keeping warm and the risk of ill-health. Smoking chimneys after working hours and at weekends would have been a clear signal that the warehouse was being used for purposes other than business, and would have resulted in discovery. Lack of warmth would have increased the chances and effects of illness, and, at a less dangerous level, there was no escape from the enervating effect of a series of cold, dreary winter weeks. At an even more basic level, try imagining the cumulative result of being cooped up with seven other people in small rooms, with the windows shut or barely open, the air stale from the coal fire (during working hours), the damp and draughts inherent in an old waterfront building, the poor supply of warm clothes (or even clothes that fitted – 1 May 1943), the cold floors and the heavy condensation that must have built up on walls and windows. The winter conditions must have been appalling, and it was no wonder that the whole group anticipated their effect by falling prey to depression. When we first read that Anne took tranquillizers (16 September 1943), we are shocked to think of her vibrant nature being forced to such measures, and then shocked again as we realize that she obviously took them with her parents' consent. There was simply no other way to cope, and it is important to be aware of the grinding, relentless pressure of the situation.

A more dangerous worry was the awareness that V.M. (see glossary section 6) was posing a threat to the secrecy of the annexe (p. 98). A warehouseman at Travies & Co., V.M. had become suspicious that the warehouse was not empty after working hours and had taken to setting traps to establish the presence of any intruders. He would, for example, place a pencil on the edge of a table or lightly scatter flour on the floor, both of which would be difficult to avoid or even be aware of. The knowledge that danger lay so near to home would have had a very serious effect on the group's morale and would have increased any tendency to rows and depression. It is both moving and heartening to see Anne's resilience at the end of this entry (p. 99). Refusing to be defeated by the many difficulties which faced the group, she concludes with an amusing vision of Kraler creeping about in his socks to avoid V.M. It is touches like this which make the diary so valuable by conveying very naturally the courage and humour that were such a dominant part of Anne's nature.

Her courage and maturity owed much to her father's example. Otto Frank had been the managing director of Travies & Co. before going into hiding, and became the unofficial leader of the group owing to his qualities of thoughtfulness and good sense. Even he however could not always rise above the constant demands of his role as peacemaker and the effects of the permanent strain on him did not escape Anne's perceptive attention. We read (29 September and 17 October 1943) of his anger and nervous reactions when spoken to, and given the vivid description of one of the Van Daans' rows (29 October 1943), one wonders how he had found the inner resources to have maintained a veneer of control for so long.

This entry is particularly moving as Anne admits just how heavily the situation weighs on her. The penultimate paragraph (p. 101) is heavy with images of fatigue and capture; 'lead ... deadly ... hangs ... drag ... underworld' forge together into a chain of despair, echoed in the final paragraph in which the simile of a caged, mutilated song-bird suggests poignantly the extent of Anne's unhappiness. This pattern of imagery is developed as she writes with both control and power of her vision of the annexe (pp. 102–3). The conflict between darkness and light, between safety and danger, between conflict and peace, is symbolically described, and Anne concludes with a passionate plea for release and safety.

Anne's dark mood and preoccupation with the unhappiness that grew upon her and the others becomes most apparent from 16 September 1943. The earlier part of this section is given over to more usual subjects, which can be seen to fall under a very general heading of domestic matters. The first entry (23 July 1943) runs quickly through a list of wishes expressed by each member of the group for when they are free. It can be read as nothing more than a record of a quick game played to pass the time, but it is touching to see Otto Frank's concern to visit his former employee, Mr Vossen, who had been forced to retire from work because of cancer. Anne's hunger for their own home, a return to school and the freedom to go where she wishes, contrast very sharply with Mrs Van Daan's desire for cream cakes. It reveals the constant attrition she suffered from being imprisoned and it contributes to the release of her pent-up unhappiness which we see in the later half of the section.

The series of entries from 4 to 23 August 1943 (excluding the 10th) provides a full, detailed and often humorous account of the group's daily routines. It makes deceptively easy reading until one realizes how well the bald facts of, for example, peeling potatoes (18 August) are used as a basis for an entertaining and observant cameo of life in the annexe. In this case, Mr and Mrs Van Daan are the main subjects of Anne's scrutiny. Mr Van Daan's pompous and sententious attempt to coerce Anne into scraping a potato in the way he thinks best is, typically, presented through dialogue. It is as if Anne is stepping aside and letting him blunder through a performance at which we, as the audience, begin to sense the opening of a comedy of manners. Anne's role is that of a foil, setting off a process which we relish watching.

She turns her attention to his wife who, true to her flirtatious nature (see 5 February 1943), tries without success to attract Dussel's attention. It is a wonderful scene, apparently concerned with very little, and yet it presents elegantly and memorably each of the characters involved. Having nagged Anne, Van Daan is given a dose of his own medicine by his wife. We can almost feel his growing irritation as she continues to ply him with pointless questions until he erupts in anger, reverting to his native German. The scene reads exactly as one would imagine in a play, except that the stage directions ('Another moment's silence'; 'Pause' p. 54) follow rather than precede the dialogue. Does it matter if Anne's memory is entirely accurate? Not at all, for her success lies in the characterization of the two people involved. If we knew nothing else about the Van Daans, this scene would more than suffice to establish their natures and their relationship to each other. Their conversation rings true, and Anne's excited, but unobtrusive pauses for comment heighten the effect of the speeches that follow them.

Similarly, she transforms the bland sequence of preparing for bed (4 August 1943) into a lively commentary in which the tiniest details gain some significance. At half-past eleven (p. 88) Dussel's entry into their shared room takes on overtones of a mystery thriller 'door creaks ... narrow strip of light ... shuffling'. To Anne's vivid imagination, everything is potentially interesting, even if only for the purpose of being deliberately deflated with the reference to 'suspicious noises from the lavatory'. Even her use of a chamberpot (three o'clock) merits attention in the memorable simile of 'a brook from a mountain'. She has the knack of noticing what most other people would only see, and then describing or imitating what she notices with a sure eye for impressions that are rich in detail and humour. When writing on 9 August 1943 of Dussel's huge appetite and consequent trips to the lavatory, Anne's voice is lively, humorous, chatty. She shares a joke with the reader, being determined to capture the lighter side of their situation, and constantly draws upon the resources of a naturally playful and vivacious personality which relishes the laughable aspects of their lives. Peter's hunt for bread and his fruitless chase of Mouschi reveals this perfectly (p. 96). The boy and the cat are presented as rivals in a mock dispute ('Mouschi spits, Peter sighs') while Anne, always alert for the unusual, stands entranced in the doorway.

Her attention is not only turned towards the comic or the solemn aspects of their lives. There is time too for a more reflective mood, and her portrait of her father as he reads and tries vainly to share his pleasure in his book with his wife is fond and moving (23 August). His 'reading wrinkle' (pp. 94 and 97) is obviously a characteristic Anne finds endearing, and she refers at various times throughout this section to 'Pim's' selfless and inspirational nature.

The final entry (11 November 1943) in some ways mirrors the whimsical style of the first one (23 July). Anne recalls her joy at receiving her fountain-pen (compare this with her delight in the dress shoes Miep bought her for a treat – 10 August 1943), and while upset at its 'cremation' she finds the spirit to rejoice that it has met with the fate she wants for herself. The story is symbolic of Anne's determination to search for something positive no matter how unhappy the circumstances.

Glosary Section 6

p. 85 **Fokker's** German aeroplane factory – an obvious target for British bombers.

p. 85 **Mussolini** Leader of the Italian Fascist party and dictator of Italy – ally of Hitler.

p. 90 **Mr. Van Senten** Miep's husband. An Amsterdam social worker and active member of the Dutch resistance.

p. 91 **A Danaidean vessel** Reference to Greek mythology. The Danaides were the fifty daughters of Danaus, King of Argos. To escape a prophecy that he would be killed by his son-in-law, Danaus instructed his daughters to slay their husbands on their wedding night. They were punished for this in Hades by being compelled to fill with water a large cask which had a hole in the bottom – hence the comparison with Peter's appetite.

p. 93 **Westertoren clock bell ... taken away** Presumably to be melted down to be used in making weapons of war.

p. 95 **Donnerwetter – noch-einmal!** Loosely, "ceaseless torrent".

p. 98 **The *Internationale*** Famous international communist song, played to celebrate the overthrow of the Fascists, political opponents of Communists.

p. 98 **V.M.** When Otto Frank decided to publish Anne's diary after her death, he used these initials to protect the identity of the Travies' warehouseman who was strongly suspected of having informed the German authorities of the annexe and its Jewish inhabitants. A clear example of Mr Frank's generosity and fairness.

Assignments Sections 5 and 6

1 Following assignment 5, Sections 3 and 4, do some background reading on Mussolini and the relationship between the Germans and Italians in World War II. Not essential, but relevant and especially useful for history students.

2 Creative writing. Building on the previous diary assignments (no. 2 sections 1 and 2, 3 and 4) try writing one long entry in which you concentrate on a difficult or oppressive situation. Write from your own experience and as Anne did, try to find the dividing line between moaning and describing. (Four hundred–eight hundred words.)

3 Anne clearly loved books and kept a record of her reading. Write a personal response (not the same as a review) of something that you have read which has made some impact on you. Try to avoid the word 'good' and look critically at the nature of your text as Anne did (29 October 1942; 12 March 1943; 29 July 1943). (Three hundred–six hundred words.)

4 Dussel and the Van Daans are clearly important figures in the diary. Work through from where they appear to the end of section 6 (11 November 1943) and note when and for what reason they are mentioned. This is important revision and will help you to establish the pattern of events clearly.

Section 7 17 November 1943–24 January 1944

There is now a marked change in the nature of Anne's concerns. Although she still refers to the occasional difficulties between people and includes a certain amount of general news and chat, there are two main areas which to a large extent break new ground. She writes with considerable self-doubt and guilt about her relationships with people close to her, and then deals very openly with her own burgeoning sexuality, demonstrating a curious blend of naïvety and innate wisdom. It is a fascinating section, full of insight and reason, yet fuelled by a passionate and urgent need to understand and improve herself.

The first entry (17 November 1943) is much along the lines of what we are used to. Difficulties caused by the absence of Elli and Koophuis are touched on briefly, as is Margot's correspondence course in Latin. There is also an uncomfortable atmosphere arising from a dispute between Mr Van Daan and Dussel, which casts a cloud over the first anniversary of the latter's arrival in the annexe. Dussel's intransigence and ungracious refusal of what could have been a celebration prompts a very apt quotation which reminds us of Anne's earlier comments about his childish nature (13 July 1943).

Her dislike of him takes a more active form of expression in the very candid entry for 22 December 1943. Lying in bed with flu, Anne is mortified when Dussel, a dentist and therefore trained in medicine, tries to sound her chest. When we consider the substantial interest she shows in sexual matters in this section, it is hardly surprising that she reacts with disgust and feels that Dussel is usurping the intimacy she would accord a lover (p. 108). The statement catches the reader by surprise for although Anne has mentioned boys before, such a direct reference to lovemaking contrasts strongly with anything she has written before and prepares us for her open acknowledgement of sexual interest a little later on.

Dussel's failure to celebrate his first year in the annexe contrasts with the enthusiastic celebration of St Nicholas' Day when Anne and her father collaborated in preparing surprise gifts for the others (6 December 1943). In accordance with their family tradition of poems for birthdays (13 June 1943), a seasonal poem is prepared and the atmosphere lightens. Similarly, Anne delights in the novelty of preparing for Christmas (22 and 27 December) and tells enthusiastically of her brooch, 'lovely, but indescribable' (p. 108) and Miep's Christmas cake (p. 109). In the face of the tragedy all around them, it was clearly felt that religious differences should be abandoned in favour of seizing on any chance to lift morale and escape the rows and depression that had become so common. The short evocative final paragraph for 22 December condenses the inconveniences faced by the group into a terse list of discomforts which were too depressing to dwell on at that time. Their effect is evident in the pessimism of the next entry.

We must keep remembering that Anne was only fourteen and a half at this time. She wants more than anything else the joy of 'feeling young' (p. 109) and feels perhaps more keenly than any of her companions the absence of ordinary pleasures. We think again of that image of a caged song-bird (p. 101) and we marvel at her fortitude. She is caught in an impossible quandary; she knows intellectually that she should be grateful for her physical safety, but her inner need for 'rollicking fun' cannot be satisfied with such cold comfort. Her unhappiness is obviously aggravated by hunger and the oppressive influence of the Van Daans (15 January 1944), but it is the constant confinement which weighs most heavily on her.

This may account to some extent for Anne's visions of her school-friend Lies and her maternal grandmother 'Granny' (27 November and 29 December 1943). On the one hand, her penitential appeals to Lies (27 November) may appear excessively morbid and self-punishing. She accuses herself of possessiveness and of neglecting even to think of her friend, but it is hard to believe that these errors would by themselves have provoked such a storm of self-criticism. The very form of the letter emphasizes the confusion and unhappiness of its writer; paragraphs begin with passionate exclamations redolent of desperation – 'Oh, God ... Oh, Lies ... Good Lord' (p. 106), and in the middle of blurting out her anguished incomprehension she stops abruptly as she realizes Lies has not been in her thoughts for a long time. Anne is clearly racked with guilt which ultimately arises from a profound questioning of the ways of Providence. Why, she feels, should she be safe when Lies and many of their other Jewish friends had been arrested by the Gestapo and sent to concentration camps? (9 October 1942). The simplistic answer, which would have been unacceptable to Anne's firm religious belief, was that Lies had been unlucky. Belief in God precludes any notion of luck, but it also raises disturbing questions about justice and the very nature of God which evade even sophisticated theological inquiry. For someone of Anne's age and in her situation, emotionally weakened by some seventeen months of fear and frequent unhappiness, it is wholly understandable that she should express this huge area of confusion through the more manageable issue of a jealous friendship.

Writing again on 29 December 1943, Anne's loneliness and unhappiness spill onto the page in an uneasy flux of unanswerable questions, self-criticism and despondent compassion. The theme of her need for one special person in whom she can confide is raised again (look back to her reason for starting the diary – 20 June 1942) in the context of a sudden apprehension of how lonely her grandmother must have been. The tone of the passage echoes that written on 27 November. It is shot through with pity for Lies' present situation and remorse for what she sees as her own ingratitude to God. Every line expresses profound uncertainty and misery. This is no doubt heightened by the prevailing dejection in the annexe, but it is also traceable to an inner emptiness which can only be filled by a special relationship with someone who can talk with her about things 'outside the common round' (p. 14).

Her search for this special friend is to some extent prompted by the distance between her and her mother. In contrast to her earlier feelings of hostility towards her mother, Anne regrets her former anger and appreciates that they are both responsible for the fracture in their relationship. The entry of 2 January 1944 examines closely Anne's own attitude. It is a forceful and analytical piece of writing, an honest assessment of how mistakes were made on both sides. The passage is unusual, as there is absolutely no element of defensiveness or reluctance to shoulder her share of the blame, and it therefore establishes even more firmly our impressions of her generous nature. It also reinforces the fact that she is interested in the truth, no matter how uncomfortable it may be to face. Her powers of observation and organization joined forces with a very mature ability to subject herself to a rigorous process of self-criticism. The letter reads beautifully; no words are wasted, and while no easy answer to the problem is forthcoming, there is a sense of peace in her final resolution to spare her mother any further anguish.

This new gentleness, a product both of Anne's developing maturity and her determination to reject anything that is less than the truth, gains further moral stature in the long introspective account of her feelings for her mother and Margot (12 January 1944). At fourteen, she is able to identify accurately the intellectual gap between herself and her mother, but speaks with a kindness devoid of any scorn. She now even finds it possible to see the Van Daans in a less hostile light (22 January 1944). As a result of her recent dream (27 November 1943), she has become more able to cope with life in the annexe because, however galling it might be at times, it is infinitely better than the fate suffered by Lies and her other Jewish friends. She is also able for the first time to step outside the bounds of family loyalty. She admits that the Van Daans are perhaps not as bad as she has previously felt and also that her mother has been partly responsible for the arguments. The dream has had a great effect on her and she now stands convinced of the need to make amends for as many mistakes as she can. Anne also sees lucidly how different she is from Margot, who appears to have a far less fretful and restless nature than hers, and she appreciates that Margot's placid nature would inevitably make her more appealing or approachable in her mother's eyes.

In a further wave of self-understanding in the same entry, she reveals her unusual ability to step outside her own immediate concern and to see herself as a stranger would (p. 119). She remembers as a child feeling distanced from even her close family and recalls with startling vividness how she would attempt to make allowances for her mother's apparent lack of warmth. Inevitably, lacking at that time the understanding that informs these letters, Anne's childish attempts to gain some demonstration of love from her mother were bound to fail. There is considerable pathos in the picture of the little girl 'wearing a pensive expression' (p. 120); we can only conclude that in the absence of a close relationship with her mother, Anne increasingly felt the need to talk at a deeply personal level with a close friend. Kitty was an agent of emotional release, but for genuine fulfilment Anne could only be satisfied with a real person.

Almost inevitably, despite their very different natures and

interests, Anne and Peter Van Daan were bound at some time to strike up a close friendship. A little younger than Peter, but intellectually and socially his superior, Anne lacks anyone else with whom she can really relax and share her thoughts. She reveals in her fascinated description of Peter (6 January 1944) the possibility of some feeling other than mere companionship, although she is quick to assert that theirs is a platonic relationship based solely on friendship. The situation may have given rise to her subsequent dream (p. 116) of her old flame, Peter Wessel, and her writing slides into an unusually maudlin account of her memories.

This gives way to the next entry (7 January 1944) and we are treated to an account of Anne's fervent affection for Peter Wessel. Her feelings are self-searching and far removed from what would normally be understood by a crush. We are startled when she confesses that her father's good-morning kiss aroused her longing for her old boyfriend, and are reminded of her passionate nature. This is openly considered in a sexual context at the end of the entry as she affirms her own understanding of desire.

The second half of her letter of 5 January discusses very openly her growing sexual feelings, even to the extent of committing to paper her fascination with images of naked women and the compulsion she felt to share some form of physical intimacy with a girlfriend. It is important to realize that this is not a revelation or confession of lesbian tendencies; her love for Peter Wessel gives the lie to that. What it does do is to delineate the strength of Anne's sexual awareness, of her fascination with the changes in her body, and we become aware of how far she has grown away from the childishly flirtatious girl of just eighteen months ago (see the entry for 20 June 1942).

Having adjusted our view of Anne to absorb this new insight into her complex character, we are thrown off balance again as she tells of how she accompanied Peter (Van Daan) to the warehouse to establish the sex of the warehouse cat Moffi. At this point her curiosity is impersonal – biological rather than sexual – as is the subsequent conversation between her and Peter about the facts of life. She clearly finds Peter's matter-of-fact examination of Moffi's 'male organs' reassuring in its absence of anything other than the wish to prove a point, and we conclude the section by realizing that Peter has in the most unconventional way begun to win Anne's respect and interest.

Glossary Section 7

p. 105 *Der Mann bat einen grossen Geist*
Und ist so klein von Tatem! Possibly a quotation from Goethe, whom she was reading at the time.

p. 105 **Lies** Presumably Lies Goosens, a schoolfriend of Anne's. See pp. 13 and 14.

p. 166 **Peter ... Wessel ... my darling Peter** See pp. 13 and 20.

p. 118 **Peter** Peter Wessel.

p. 124 **Bredero** Seventeenth-century writer based in Amsterdam, famous for comical drama.

Section 8 27 January 1944–6 March 1944

Just as the last section concentrated on Anne's growing sexual awareness, we now read of her increasing fondness for Peter Van Daan. Before examining the section in detail though, it is necessary to clarify as far as we can Anne's attitude towards him. It would be a serious mistake to assume that her open revelations of sexual interest now govern her view of her relationship with Peter, or indeed, that they lead to any form of sexual activity. Leaving aside the impossibility of such a situation developing in the cramped quarters of the annexe, we would be guilty of a very serious misreading of Anne's nature and her emotional needs if we thought that she would allow such a betrayal of her family, her faith and her ideals. It is perfectly clear as we read through this section that Anne is deeply pleased at the knowledge of Peter's growing interest in her, but she can only permit the development of their relationship within the context of her principles and her need for a companion who can truly share with her. There is certainly a strongly romantic tinge to her comments about Peter, especially towards the end of the section, but underlying this is a fundamental need for companionship and 'fellowship' (p. 132). The expression of this need stretches back to the earliest part of the diary and one major cause of it, the absence of a real bond between her and her mother, has been discussed in Section 5.

If Anne's interest in Peter had been sexually prompted, the last entry in section 7 in which they examined Moffi's 'male organs' (24 January 1944) might well have led to some intense writing in which sex played a significant part. Anne obviously understood the facts of life and given her absolute commitment to writing about everything she felt was important, she would surely have seen that incident as a springboard for such a train of thought.

In contrast to this however, we find her only three days later writing about family trees and film stars. She enthuses over the fascination of hunting through the past and also refers to her continued hard work in English and other studies. She comments with pleasure on her encyclopaedic knowledge of the cinema and only half-seriously complains about the reception she gets if she tries out a different hair-style. This is all very ordinary, innocent stuff – there is no dwelling on more secretive thoughts and the incident with Moffi has been replaced by new topics of interest.

Similarly, her return to older concerns on 28 January is innocuous and is written with her customary attention to detail. She complains about the tedium of life in the annexe, arising from the fact that none of them has anything new or interesting to say, and humorously criticizes Dussel who 'twaddles on' about a number of well-worn trivialities. She even excuses herself to Kitty for the lack of new information, and uses a vivid if unflattering image of 'old cows' to describe their subjects of conversation.

This is purely a temporary line of thought and Anne soon gives the lie to any self-accusation of tediousness by becoming immersed in genuinely interesting material. She praises the invaluable contribution that Dutch resistance movements are making to the lives of people like themselves who have gone 'underground'. She speaks gratefully of their own helpers and correctly sees that their constant efforts to keep cheerful are a heroic attempt to sustain the morale of the group. War gossip such as the football match and illegal issue of ration books to people in hiding (p. 127) is faithfully recorded and there is no hint that Peter Van Daan occupies any special place in her thoughts.

The long entry for 3 February continues to dwell on the war. By 1944, the Allied forces were making substantial progress against German troops in Europe. There was much expectation that Holland would be invaded, the Germans would surrender or be defeated and the Dutch people would be liberated. The effects of an Allied invasion form the basis of the conversations which Anne records in this entry. As before, it is hardly likely that she would have been able to sustain a verbatim report; what is important is that she captures the various moods and attitudes of the speakers. Their comments are broken down into two main areas; firstly, there is some amused speculation as to how they would cope in the event of the Germans flooding large tracts of the country. Flooding was a traditional Dutch defence against invasion and until the German bomber and paratroop attack in 1940 had been a successful means of holding an aggressor at bay while maintaining military neutrality. It clearly presented no terrors for the refugees who indulged in a series of absurd suggestions (pp. 127–8) and saw it as an excuse for some light-hearted nonsense, although Anne was aware that the reality could be difficult and dangerous.

The second area of response to the possible German action in the event of invasion is more serious and culminates in a sombre reminder of the mass slaughter of Jews by the Nazi forces (pp. 128–30). The conversation between Henk Van Senten and the men of the annexe presents two opposing views of the Germans: Henk tends to give them the benefit of the doubt, while the German Jews (Otto Frank, Van Daan and Dussel) feel strongly in the light of their experiences in Germany that there is no cruelty the Nazis will not stoop to, especially when desperate.

Anne's well-established method of using direct speech is most effective here. We have seen it used to good comic effect before, but it now invests the discussion about the future of Dutch Jews with a dark conviction that reminds us of how much danger the group is still in. An invasion would not necessarily have guaranteed their automatic freedom and safety; it could have had exactly the opposite effect.

It would appear that Anne had no part in these discussions (p. 130). This was not due to a lack of informed ideas on her part, but to a fatalistic acceptance of the possibility of death. She is not depressed or suicidal, but she has reached very early in her life an understanding of the truth that the only thing one can do is to live one day at a time. She knows that to do anything else would only result in sinking herself (and probably a number of the others) into despair and resolves to address such unpleasant thoughts only as and when it is actually necessary.

This is a very natural reaction when one has lost virtually all control over the direction of one's life. All that can be done is to drift with the situation, but for Anne such a passive admission of helplessness has a price to pay and she cries desperately 'for freedom, for friends ...' (p. 130). The tension created by the arrival of spring, symbolic of new life and new hope, in a situation where death can be the result of a careless footstep, is too poignant for Anne to bear and she collapses into a series of confused statements whose very lack of organization emphasizes her condition.

We are relieved on reading the next day that Anne has risen above her unhappiness to a sense of elation, caused by her awareness of Peter Van Daan's interest in her. To date, their friendship has to all intents and purposes been platonic, but there is now a very different sense of a special closeness which Anne finds utterly delightful (13 February 1944). The rare incoherence that her feelings produce is very well captured, but the effect is balanced through her recognition that she has to exert some self-control over them. Another example of how strongly the effect of Peter's new regard for her has affected her is apparent in her desperate wish to 'be alone', to savour the excitement of her new place in Peter's life.

She is now able to reveal a new side of her nature. The main impression that we have of Anne is of a lively, talkative, impatient girl with plenty of ideas and views about a number of subjects. We now see her as a sympathetic listener, able to draw out the uncommunicative Peter (14 February). Although she is aware of his special feelings for her and enjoys them very much, it is revealing that at the end of the entry she refers to 'fellowship' – not romance. She is no starry-eyed adolescent vicariously living out the plot of one of her favourite love films (read her comment about his dishonesty – 16 February 1944). Rather, she senses beneath Peter's romantic interest a need similar to her own, the need for affection and understanding. When he praises her for her sound choice of potatoes (16 February 1944) her pleasure comes from the sense of Peter's wish to do the right thing in her eyes. He is as yet very far from being a lover; he is instead 'a helper' (12 January 1944), a sharer of confidences and a friend.

Given Anne's vision of their friendship, it is hardly surprising that she resents her mother's suspicions about the time she spends in Peter's room (18 February 1944). Edith Frank would have been better aware than her daughter of the dangers inherent in such a situation, but Anne is alienated by the thought that her mother would suspect her of anything but proper behaviour. It may also have been the case that in addition to resenting the aspersions cast upon her morality, Anne would have felt very keenly that her protective, sharing relationship with Peter would have been sullied by such suspicions.

She is a complex girl and her friendship with Peter demonstrates this very clearly. While on the one hand she talks in measured terms of life having become more 'pleasant' since she grew closer to him (18 February 1944), we find her weeping the next day because she is unsure of his feelings for her. And yet even in the middle of this emotional release, her primary desire is that Peter should see her as someone in whom he can 'confide' (p. 135). Despite her emotional confusion about Peter, Anne is very clear-sighted about what she sees as fruitful in their relationship. Trust, encouragement and sympathy are elevated high above any precocious romantic interest. The latter element is apparent, but only gains definition in the context of other more substantial qualities upon which rests her self-respect.

That Anne values her own self-respect is indisputable. The closing sentence of the addition to her letter of 23 February 1944 is a form of personal creed, not in conflict with her religious faith, but an individual appreciation of what she finds most satisfying. In her eyes 'the heavens, nature and God' (p. 136) are coequal expressions of spiritual blessing and we remember her anguished outburst about the impression spring makes on her (12 February 1944). Here (p. 137) she concentrates on trying to show how essential nature is as a means of achieving inner peace and purity. She writes lyrically of the natural scene outside Peter's attic, and even when alone with him her thoughts are of 'sunshine' and 'cloudless skies' (23 February 1944).

Although there is a temporary hiatus in her examination of her relationship with Peter owing to a burglary in the warehouse below (1 March 1944) and the attendant risk of discovery, Anne disposes of this crucial matter in one entry. She writes superbly as always, relating Van Daan's thoughts as he discovered traces of criminal entry, and she speculates in a series of dramatic questions about the key issues of the matter. This is however merely a concession to the importance of the event and she soon returns to the subject of Peter (2 March 1944). Part of his appeal is that like her he is distanced from his mother and is very sensitive (27 February 1944). She finds in him a blend of friend and ally in the face of what she perceives as adult persecution (2 March 1944) and is very pleased when he praises her father, the one adult for whom she has real affection and respect. As she shares in Peter's emotional life, she finds herself beginning to respond romantically (28 February and 3 March 1944) – the order of events is important.

The last three entries of the section (3, 4 and 6 March 1944) consolidate our awareness of her affection for Peter. Even after declaring that he has joined Peter Wessel in the romantic shores of Anne's mind (28 February), she is still able to examine her feelings carefully and sensibly (3 March). She is near to being in love, but refuses to be swept into any indiscretion of thought or action.

Glossary Section 8

p. 125 **the English Home Service** BBC broadcast which Anne uses to develop her English.

p. 125 *Cinema and Theatre* Presumably a magazine for film fans.

p. 126 **the underground movement** General term for secret Dutch organizations aimed at subverting all aspects of German control.

p. 127 **flooding** Traditional Dutch method of defence.

p. 129 **Per pedes apostolorum** 'On foot, like the apostles'.

p. 129 **Goebbels** German minister of Public Enlightenment and Propaganda.

p. 131 **Immortal Music of the German Masters** Propagandist programme broadcast by official radio. See glossary section 5.

p. 133 **Dutch East Indies** Now Indonesia, formerly a wealthy Dutch colony rich in natural resources.

p. 138 **Kolen & Co.** Fictitious version of cover name given to Travies & Co. while the Franks were in hiding.

p. 141 **Oma** Dutch word for grandmother.

p. 143 **my conquest** i.e. of her own nature.

Assignments Sections 7 and 8

1 Following assignment 5, Sections 3 and 4, read and make appropriate notes on how the Germans made life very difficult for the Dutch Jews between the time of the invasion (May 1940) and summer 1942, just before the Franks went into hiding.

2 An imitative piece. Rather than writing for yourself, add an

entry anywhere in these two sections. Either develop existing subject matter or add something completely new. Aim as far as possible to copy Anne's 'voice'. Refer to things you think she might have done.

3 Anne's older sister Margot is only mentioned from time to time, possibly because of her undemonstrative nature. Write either a) a letter from her to a distant relative in a safe country in which she not only tells of the situation in Holland and their lives in the annexe, but comments freely about her younger sister.

or b) a long conversation between her and Anne about, say, Peter, their parents, the future, the books they have been reading and anything else that you think would arise.

Section 9 7 March 1944–28 March 1944

Anne's thoughts continue to be focused closely on Peter, but there is now a quietness and deep maturity rarely apparent in the preceding section. Her relationship with Peter has pulled her out of a destructive circle of boredom and aimlessness, and while their friendship creates its own problems, it also provides Anne with the impetus to see life more from other people's points of view as her attention is taken away from herself and directed towards another person. This is not to say that she had been selfish and egotistical, but there is no doubt that the physically and emotionally cramped conditions of life in the annexe would not have helped her achieve a balanced perspective of herself in relation to other people. The finding of a real friend is for Anne one of life's most generous gestures, as she is able to savour for the first time the joy of being able to share her feelings closely and confidently with the sort of friend she has always wished for.

An apparently small item at the end of the long opening entry for 7 March 1944 provides an important hint in relation to Anne's search for a confidential friend. We have seen before that her relationship with her mother is uncertain and lacks the roots of common understanding, and that she is therefore denied natural access to one of the deepest human relationships. Here however new light is thrown upon what might have been seen merely as a polished evocation of the common situation of conflict between parent and child. This time, without anger or bitterness, Anne puts her finger precisely on a significant and insurmountable difference between her and her mother. Anne is sensitive, highly intelligent and has a profound religious faith. These three elements inform her statement (p. 146) that no matter how difficult or unhappy a period one's life might be in, there will always be 'some beauty left'. It may reside in apparently simple things, such as the appreciation of nature or even just a sunny day, or it may result from an inner awareness of oneself. This is a profound and courageous observation, perhaps especially so for a young person. It reveals that its writer will always be able to overcome obstacles because immediate difficulties or inconvenience will never be able to break through her wall of certainty about the purpose in life. A genuine religious faith can never be permanently overcome by unhappiness. There will always be, as Anne so strongly argues, something good which remains intact and which one can turn to for consolation and inspiration.

In contrast, her mother clearly lacks this practical faith and views life negatively, thankful only to have escaped a worse situation. The difference between them is absolute; one is buoyant and grateful, the other entrenched in a cramped posture of mind and spirit. This first entry is important for two reasons. Firstly, it is a remarkable piece of self-examination – never maudlin or self-indulgent – but descriptive and, to some extent, even dispassionate. The Anne Frank under consideration is distanced from Anne Frank the writer – 'What is left of this girl?' (p. 144) and her past behaviour is scrutinized closely and honestly. Her commitment to truth is evident when she describes herself as generous and never conceited. This is not an ego-boosting exercise drawn from blindness to her own faults, but the result of a candid appraisal of her good and bad points. She is concerned to state the truth, not to flatter herself or to exercise a transparent piece of false humility.

The second paragraph of the entry is a brief, but comprehensive survey of her past nature and it is worth nothing that she applies neither praise nor criticism to herself. It is simply a statement about a person who happens to be herself, and who is now seen to have been 'superficial' (p. 144). She recognizes that she was attractive to others and a flirt, but in keeping with her controlled handling of her developing friendship with Peter, she now understands that 'followers' and 'admirers' are worthless and that what she wants and needs are genuine friends.

The second half of the entry examines lucidly and objectively the nature of her changing behaviour over the last two years, with particular attention paid to the reasons why she went through a long period of unhappiness and conflict with the adults. She traces the maturing process she has undergone, identifying each stage and condition clearly, but without committing any excesses either of self-criticism or evasion of the truth. Her sense of her own value has been refined and defined. She no longer feels it necessary to entertain or provoke others in a bid to achieve recognition. Her understanding of what is valuable in life has become much clearer, and with this new awareness, her old self is painlessly consigned to the past. A new Anne faces the future, rejoicing in each stage of her love for Peter. The fourth paragraph from the end (pp. 145–6) is startling in the controlled delicacy of its vision of 'all that is exquisite and fine'. It is no conjuration of distorted rapture born out of sudden access of high spirits, but a sincere statement of Anne's hard-won wisdom. She has fought for over eighteen months to gain some measure of understanding and control over her feelings, and is now able to enjoy the rewards inherent in having to some extent come to terms with her own nature.

Her moments of peace and inspiration do not however leave her immune to the demands of the daily pressures of physical privation and inner conflict. She is still subject to the frustration arising from an incomplete and uncertain relationship with Peter, and with no other means of release at difficult times, she immerses herself in her diary in order to be able to appear as cheerful as usual when in public (p. 147). The entry for 12 March 1944 is not so much an examination as an outpouring of her feelings. She is denied constant access to Peter, the one person to whom she feels she can talk openly, for fear of outstaying her welcome, and her thoughts move restlessly from one topic to another. Even Margot, for all her kindness and intelligence, is of limited value to Anne in helping her to achieve lasting inner peace. With a degree of insight to be admired whatever her age might be, Anne realizes that Margot 'lacks the ease necessary for conducting deep discussions' (p. 147); through this we see a little more closely the quality of Anne's mind as she realizes at fourteen that profound talk can harmonize perfectly with humour. She is also able to see herself through Margot's eyes, and understands perfectly that their forced intimacy paradoxically results in less real companionship than might have been the case in more normal circumstances.

This ability to release excessive pressure via the safety valve of her diary is for Anne the 'brightest spot' (p. 151) of her difficult life. This statement is important because it emphasizes the extent of her anxiety while demonstrating the need of a born writer to make sense of life through the written word. She again examines her own feelings and behaviour without self-pity (16 March 1944), but the quick-fire battery of questions in the penultimate paragraph is an open statement of her need for Peter. The difficult process of maturing, seen in the uneven development of her involvement with Peter, is highlighted in the entry for 17 March as Anne discusses one particular obstacle in her path to adulthood. She feels that although she knows herself to be independent, rational, capable and responsible, she is still subjected to forms of address by the adults that are more suited to a child. Her complaint is not a restatement of the fretful complaints that cropped up so often during the entries for 1942 and 1943, in relation to several different issues; it indicates instead a more fundamental conflict between her view of herself as a young woman and the reluctance or inability of the adults to respond to the change. Twenty-one months have now passed since the diary was started – a short time for an adult, but a period of rapid and intense development for Anne, especially in the hothouse of the annexe. She yearns to abandon the practices of childhood – the frequent kisses, the pet names, the early bedtimes, the vetted literature – and even the compliant Margot protests against what she sees as an intrusive degree of concern for their health (p. 152).

Margot is brought into the foreground of the diary in the entries for 20 and 22 March 1944. She has been a shadowy figure referred to occasionally and in passing, never occupying much of Anne's attention in the diary. According to Miep Gies (Van Senten) in *Anne Frank Remembered*, Margot was very different to Anne – quiet, passive, undemonstrative. Characteristically, she appears in the diary purely via letters exchanged between her and Anne. It is interesting to think for a moment about why the letters were written. There are hints that they had talked about Peter, but that the issue of a possible close friendship between him and Margot was too embarrassing or difficult to manage directly. The letters are also very polished, rather formal affairs, very ordered and reasonable and brimful of generosity. They illustrate perfectly not only both sisters' facility with pen and paper, but perhaps also suggest through their very courtesy the absence of a strong, relaxed bond between them. This is of course arguable. What is irrefutable is the kindness each shows to the other, seen in Anne's compassion for what she imagines is Margot's 'terrible pain' (p. 154) and Margot's desire to set Anne's mind at rest by assuring her that she has no special interest in Peter. There is no catty attempt by Anne to warn Margot away, and no patronizing response from Margot to her little sister. Each holds the other in high regard and is able to discuss disinterestedly her attitude to Peter.

Anne's ability to distance herself from emotional excess is another index of her maturity. She writes with a new humility and tolerance of her mother (p. 155), accepting the scolding she received, and vows to treat her with more consideration. Her maturity is also evident in the disciplined, lucid account of 19 March when she tells of the new confidence that has developed between her and Peter. Her main delight is in the fact that they have been able to pour out many of their deepest concerns to each other, and to find out that Peter thinks and feels as she does. The traditional adolescent complaint of feeling alienated from parents is shared, and there are hints of romantic interest in her reference to his laughing eyes.

Any romantic possibilities are carefully controlled by Anne, and her friendship and growing intimacy with Peter do not stray beyond the bounds of propriety. She feels able to approach her father to ask if her visits upstairs to Peter's room are acceptable, and there is no indication that either side can see any problems, despite the reservations of the two mothers. Anne admits to Kitty that she is 'mad about him' (p. 162), but her feelings are a blend of fondness, admiration and a teenage crush, not a sexual hunger which would have barred her from discussing their friendship with Pim and Margot. As in the entry for 16 March, the strength and consequent confusion of her happiness results in a rushed series of questions, but her inherent good sense and sure conviction of how to behave govern the flow and direction of her response to Peter.

Although much of this section is about Anne's love for Peter and her growing understanding of herself, there is still time for less personal matters and a reminder of her talent for humorous mimicry. The entry for 14 March begins with a brief portrayal of the hardships suffered by the group owing to the lack of food caused by the capture of their food suppliers. The long established intimacy with Kitty allows Anne to launch straight into a summary of lack of coupons, black-market milk, the stink of old kale, bad eggs, rotten plums and diseased potatoes. In order to cheer herself up, Anne then writes a series of brief monologues which capture vividly the nature of each speaker (pp. 148–9).

The situation eases just over a week later when their food supplies are restored (23 March 1944), but a crackle of resentment is provoked by what Anne sees as a heavy-handed response from the adults to her friendship with Peter. She dismisses Van Daan's and Dussel's rudeness (p. 158) with quick contempt, and sees clearly into the reason for her mother's reticence about her and Peter. She records a charming conversation between them in which Peter's sincere and innocent flattery contrasts directly with the adults' disapproval or innuendo. The only one to escape criticism is Otto Frank, whose gentle teasing inspires a humorous sally from Anne (p. 158).

Writing on 27 March, Anne's subject is ostensibly politics and war news. Apart from her approval of Churchill's oratory however, her interest is caught by the adults' response to the latest news broadcasts. She talks slightly of the 'old geese' (p. 160) and their insatiable desire for more and more political argument, but her humour robs the words of any offence.

The closing paragraphs (pp. 160–1) illustrate perfectly how a peaceful scene of domestic harmony is shattered by what turns out to be a reassuring broadcast. Anne resorts to a despairing 'Brr,brr,brr . . .' and leaves us to imagine the subsequent uproar.

Glossary Section 9

p. 147 **people . . . food coupons . . . caught** The refugees in the annexe would have illegally received food coupons smuggled in by sympathizers.

p. 148 **"under the counter"** On the black market.

p. 149 **not in Poland** Polish Jews suffered terribly. Some two and a half million are thought to have been murdered in German concentration camps.

p. 149 **Enfin** Finally.

p. 152 **"skew-wiff"** Disordered.

p. 159 **Um Gottes Willen** A mild expletive: 'For God's sake!'

p. 160 **Wehrmacht** German Army.

p. 160 **our beloved Winston Churchill** Anne refers to Britain's
wartime Prime Minister as a symbolic leader of the allied countries.

Section 10 29 March 1944–27 April 1944

In contrast to her understandable impatience with the mono-
tonous round of political talk to which she is an unwilling audience, Anne has an informed and compassionate view of the
effects of the war on her people. The first entry (29 March 1944)
bemoans the poverty and consequent crime that has become
such a marked feature of Dutch life (p. 163). It is a dark picture
of a whole country struggling to stay alive by almost any means,
the only spark of optimism residing in the increased number of
acts of sabotage against the Germans.

Most of the diary has been taken up by issues that are either
personal or related to the life of the annexe. This quick pano-
ramic glimpse of life outside, however, sets the group's hardships in some sort of context, and it is not unfair to think that
Anne drew some of the inspiration which is apparent in this
section from her awareness of just how bad life was for all Dutch
people, Jewish or not. She concludes a long list of items which
form their diet (3 April 1944) by affirming that no one in the
annexe has starved, and that their meals are often enjoyed. The
description of the different types of food is, as with any situation
she tells of, rich in detail enlivened by snatches of personal
comment. Study this letter and work out just how Anne manages
to avoid falling into the trap of simply writing a list. She is never
satisfied either with a bland summary of a situation (e.g., 'Our
diet is boring'), but deftly arranges specific items of information
into a very readable narrative. She does not complain of the
conditions, and once more we are reminded of her strength of
will.

Anne's determination not to give in to the troubles of annexe
life stems partly, then, from her understanding of what life is
like outside, coupled with the obvious fact that to put a foot out
of doors would almost certainly be fatal. Another reason for
staying the course derives from a deep inner conviction of what

she wants to achieve in life. She emphasizes in the entry for 4 April her need for constant work so that she can become a journalist. She knows that she has some talent (p. 166), but realizes that there is a long way to go and that continued study and practice are essential if she is to achieve her aim. To say that she is ambitious would be misleading, as ambition tends to be associated with the achievement of external goals – wealth, fame, power. The impression we receive when reading this entry is very different, that Anne's desire to write is born out of an urgent need to develop what she sees as a gift from God. She rejects, not scornfully, but with the rigour of real insight, the lives that her mother and Mrs Van Daan have led, and knows that for her the life of the mind is the only life worth living.

In his novel *Out of the Silent Planet*, C. S. Lewis says that 'the love of knowledge is a kind of madness', meaning that it can be a compulsive powerful force in a person's life. This is certainly true of Anne. The irony of her passionate exclamation, 'I want to go on living even after my death!' (p. 167) is tragic, but we rejoice that her most profound desire was granted shortly after her death and that she achieved her wish to become a writer whose work influenced so many people for good.

The range of her interests is extensive and indicates clearly the direction that her life would have taken: genealogy, history, mythology, reading, history of art, films, poets, painters and writing (6 April). The world of intellectual activity had already claimed her and she affirms at the end of the very long entry for 11 April that she 'will work in the world and for mankind!' (p. 175). Such a vision of her life cannot be satisfactorily described as an ambition; it is rather a wholesale commitment to a life that will benefit others through the best means she can offer. We might stop for a moment and look back at her list of interests. Her teenage absorption with film stars lends the common touch to what might appear otherwise to be a forbidding list of stuffy learning, but she does not delude herself with empty dreams of entering the two-dimensional world of celluloid stardom. She knows that life is short and that to make the best use of one's talents is the only means of real fulfilment. (Read her short story *Dreams of Movie Stardom* in *Tales from the Secret Annexe* for an account of Anne's own feelings about this.)

For Anne, writing is both a need and a means by which she feels she can make her mark on the world. It is therapy and also fulfilment, and each entry endorses her vision of herself as a future author. We have seen before how she is able to turn a record of events into a compelling narrative (i.e. 8 July 1942) by creating suspense and by referring to a host of relevant details which serve to establish a scene firmly in the reader's imagination. The very long entry for 11 April 1944 exemplifies this process, so that we read not just an account of a very dangerous and frightening time for the refugees, but we are drawn into the situation through a host of techniques that accumulate to give us some impression of the fear and unpleasantness resulting from the attempted burglary.

The sheer length of the passage reveals how deeply it concerned Anne. They could easily have been captured when the police visited the building, and the scene impressed itself very firmly on Anne's mind. A writer less gripped by the power of words to evoke and to excite might have reduced this episode to a series of facts which were true, but which lacked any capacity to involve the reader imaginatively in what happened.

One of Anne's techniques here is to use a range of sensory experiences. A door bangs, all is quiet, the town clock strikes the quarter to the hour, footsteps are heard on the stairs (p. 169). The series of auditory impressions which gives the frightened girls and women incomplete and uncertain information about the events in the warehouse below functions dramatically; it seizes our attention, but leaves us speculating as to the significance of the sounds and any possible outcome. The lack of any embellishment or unnecessary description, the short statements and the unanswerable questions all heighten the stark sense of panic which is being controlled with difficulty.

A similar approach is used on page 170 as the refugees wait upstairs for the inevitable sequel to the burglary. The police come and even shake the bookcase which acts as a door to the hideout. The tension develops as time passes – 'but not a sound'. Footsteps are heard moving slowly towards the hideout and taut, terse questions and exclamations show to what extent Anne is caught up in the story. She needs to exorcize the fear of the event by examining it in writing, but her imagination is gripped by the drama and she cannot help but respond in the way she knows best. We can look back to her reflection of 4 April and see how justified she was in her ambition to become a writer. The grasp of details, the fluid ordering of events, the tension, the clear description – all are interwoven with apparent ease in the account of the burglary. There is no sense of strain or of any exaggeration. The writing is evocative of her feelings, but is controlled by a natural lightness of touch and sense of pace and focus. She knows that to dwell for too long, for example, on portraying the immediate symptoms of their fear will devalue its effect on paper, and she moves smoothly to a less stressful, but equally evocative account of the improvised chamber pot (p. 170). She spares no details about the effect of the fear on their natural functions, and in the face of such unsavoury details, we can only marvel at their courage and patience. Anne's purpose is of course not to dwell unnecessarily on ugliness, but the impressionistic effect of 'fear, stink, people breaking wind and always someone on the pot' (p. 171) is an unforgettable reminder of what sordid extremes the group – and hundreds like them – suffered as a result of Nazi oppression.

The horror of the burglary prompts an indignant outburst from Anne (p. 174). Her voice becomes prophetic, not just asking, but *demanding* to know the reason for the Jews' suffering. As she did with the subject of her writing on p. 167, she affirms the purpose of her existence, this time moving beyond her own ambitions and passionately declares her love for Holland and its people. She makes an even stronger profession of her Jewish faith and nationality, gaining strength and assurance from her sense of being part of the historical and spiritual process to which God has called all Jews.

The passage has been prompted by fear, but there is no sense of imbalance or hysteria. The fear has swept away the dead wood of trivialities inevitable in any diary (the handling of which has, however, resulted in some very entertaining material) and draws from Anne a concentrated statement, a creed, of her faith in God, her country and herself.

Another result of the burglary, inevitably, is to draw Anne and Peter closer together. The afternoon finds them gaining quiet comfort by sitting with their arms around each other. The lack of any romantic comment by Anne about their growing intimacy shows how deeply the burglary had shocked them. She and Peter sit close together for comfort, this early embrace a sign of trust and of the deep bond that has slowly grown between them. We remember how only a year before she would have gone to her father for comfort when in danger, and we realize that she has grown up.

She says at the end of the entry that she is 'a woman with inward strength and plenty of courage' (p. 175), a theme that has been particularly apparent in this section. Maturity is giving her perspective on their communal life in the annexe, so that she is able to come more easily to terms with its daily irritations. She is also at a deeper level gaining a firm vision of herself as a woman and as a writer, someone who will not be limited by the petty restrictions and concerns of ordinary life.

As a facet of her general development and her growing closeness to Peter, Anne waits for a measure of increased physical intimacy. She talks on 1 April of her desire for her first kiss, her feelings directed by the heightened romantic bliss she experienced in her dream of her old friend, Peter Wessel (6 January 1944). That her memory of this dream has lasted for nearly three months is an indication of the strength of her imagination and her longing for her love for Peter Van Daan to be returned. Some confusion may arise here. Which Peter is she in love with? I think that Anne's capacity for being moved by her feelings and memories, as seen in her rapturous response to her dream, must be dissociated from her involvement in an actual situation. Peter Van Daan is not a substitute for the adored Peter Wessel; rather, Anne's past experience has provided her with the emotional vocabulary by which she can define her joy in her present situation.

When the great moment finally comes (16 April 1944), the importance for Anne of the gentle intimacy preceding the kiss is apparent in her close, detailed description of the scene (p. 177). As has been said before, Anne's relationship with Peter is not a first step in sexual experimentation. Her physical closeness to Peter represents simultaneously the bridging of an emotional gap and an expression of the happiness she has found in a very close, trusting friendship. The kiss itself is nothing more than a clumsy, fleeting attempt, the innocence of which is evident in Anne's unintended humour as she tells of how she immediately rushed off – and is looking forward to her next meeting with Peter.

The next day's entry is not however given over to an extended lyrical account of their next meeting. The tone is completely different as Anne's restless mind dwells upon the situation, questioning its propriety and affirming its rightness in the light of the few opportunities for joy that their lives currently offer. Beneath the uncertainty and the desire for happiness, Anne's constant reaching out for independence is seen again as she claims the right to follow her own motives.

We see too in the closing lines that physical closeness by itself can never satisfy her. The same point is established the next day (18 April) as she recognizes the limited enjoyment to be gained from 'lying in each other's arms day in, day out' (p. 179). The old hunger for the sharing of deeply felt ideas and convictions is as strong as ever. Even though Anne rejoices in the tranquillity afforded by her new relationship with Peter (19 April) and is led to change her form of address to Kitty to 'My darling', she does not conform to any easy stereotyped image of an infatuated adolescent.

Glossary Section 10

p. 162 **Bolkestein** Gerrit Bolkestein, Minister of Education, Art and Science in the Dutch Government in London.

p. 163 **Ijmuiden** A dockside town. The bombing was heard in Amsterdam, over twenty kilometres away.

p. 164 **the Russian front** A reference to Hitler's Eastern Front in Europe, the line of battle between the German and Russian forces. In February 1943 the Russians began to push the Germans westward after the latter's unsuccessful siege of Stalingrad over the winter of 1942/43.

p. 164 **the Pruth** The river Pruth in Russia, just north of Rumania.

p. 164 **Odessa** The Russian port near the Romanian border by the Black Sea. It was the launching pad for the Russian advance against German forces into Bulgaria, Hungary and Czechoslovakia in 1944.

p. 164 **Stalin** Josef Vissarionovich Stalin (1879–1953). Following Lenin's death in 1924, Stalin, having established his position by playing one rival off against another, became the undisputed leader of the Soviet Union by 1929. In the 1930s he conducted a series of murderous purges in his own country to eliminate all opposition, real or imaginary. He was a wartime ally of Britain, France and America after 1941, following the German attacks on Russia in June 1941. Prior to this he was an ally of Hitler.

p. 164 **that dream** See 7 January 1944.

p. 166 **'Eva's Dream', 'Cady's Life'** Stories Anne wrote, now in a collection entitled *Tales from the Secret Annexe*.

p. 171 **N.S.B.** The Dutch Nazi Movement.

p. 181 **"Blurr, the Explorer"** Should read "Blurry, the Explorer". In *Tales from the Secret Annexe*.

p. 182 **Eldorado** Golden land and city, imagined by the Spanish conquerors of America. Peter refers to Anne as his treasure.

p. 182 **Thackeray** William Makepeace Thackeray (1811–1863), famous nineteenth-century novelist and man of letters. Best known for his novel *Vanity Fair* (1847–8), a study of society before and after the battle of Waterloo (1815).

p. 182 **Shem, Ham and Japheth** Noah's sons. See Genesis v, 32.

Assignments Sections 9 and 10

1 Skim-read the diary to date and note down the entries which refer to Anne's preoccupation with the need to have a close friend with whom she can share her thoughts and interests.

2 Anne has an unusual talent for looking objectively at herself and at how she has changed. Try writing about an area of your life which you now feel is past. Aim to describe fully but succinctly how you thought and behaved at that time, and indicate any change you feel has taken place. The idea is for you to experience something of the way that Anne used her diary as a means of self-examination.

3 Otto Frank seems to have a relaxed attitude to his daughter's friendship with Peter. Either make a list or write a couple of paragraphs saying why you think he seemed to encourage the situation.

Section 11 28 April 1944–25 May 1944

Although the substantial opening entry about Anne's growing physical intimacy with Peter belongs to some extent with the last section, it also has some very clear-sighted reservations about the actual possibilities of their relationship. Anne's own attitude is ambivalent. On the one hand, she feels that 'Peter has touched my emotions more deeply than anyone . . .' (p. 183), and we read of the 'wave' of feeling that overcomes her as she sits close by him (p. 182). He is by his sheer presence able to elicit powerful emotional responses from Anne, to the extent that her father now begins to regret his earlier encouragement of their friendship and feels it necessary to caution Anne against what looks like becoming an over-intense, imbalanced relationship (2 May 1944).

Characteristically, Anne does not simply give a summarized account of their conversation, but recalls it by using direct speech to lend it immediacy and impact. She could not possibly have remembered exactly what was said, but in recreating the nature of their talk she demonstrates her flair for dialogue and her ability to arrange her material into a narrative sequence that not only reads well, but convinces us of its essential truth. At the end of their conversation, for example, she is able to abandon any authorial commentary, and her version of the things they said takes on a life of its own. In this way, she breathes life into her characters and reveals again the way she can use writing to focus and order her feelings.

The extent of Pim's concern for his daughter's well-being and good name never overcomes his gentle, liberal handling of her. He is, however, very upset on receiving her letter (6 May 1944) and honestly speaks his mind to her regarding her apparent rejection of responsibility towards him and his wife (7 May). Again, and this feature is a continued aspect of Anne's writing apparent in many entries, the spoken words gain a life of their own, independent of any controlling narrative. Anne conveys the sense of his indignation and hurt most effectively through the repetition of 'you' (p. 189) in this entry, the result of which is to emphasize the extent of her debt to her parents. The substance of her letter to her father – her mother, as we know, is excluded from sharing any of Anne's confidences – forms the basis of the entry for 5 May. In this case, she writes not to reflect or report on things that have happened, but to rehearse what she feels must be said. There is a certain self-consciousness about the letter, an unusual absence of insight into Pim's motives for cautioning her, that leads her into an excess of accusation against the man who has always been at the centre of her life. She portrays herself as a noble heroine, self-sacrificing and uncomplaining, and as possessing a sureness and strength that can dispense with parental guidance. Her attitude is of course not unique, and its brittleness becomes evident two days later as she regrets passionately the impulse that prompted her to write so defensively and hurtfully (7 May).

Adolescence is traditionally a difficult time. Attitudes to oneself and to others, often parents, become blurred, and

motives are very difficult to establish. In addition to these customary problems, Anne was a very complex girl, whose unusual
demands on herself inevitably impinged on what she expected
from those around her. Life in the annexe hardly helped her to
achieve a balanced view of her companions (although her
insights were very sharp), and her fundamental need for love
and reassurance is apparent both in this episode with Pim, and
in her feelings for Peter. On the one hand she is overwhelmed
with the romantic developments between them. She is caught up
into a magical world of 'suppressed longings' and 'blissful memories' (p. 183), of heightened feelings and new emotional experience. And yet, behind and beyond her rapture, she stands back
and looks objectively at their relationship.

She is aware that Peter does not seem to experience the same
feelings that she does and she wonders about his understanding
of her (28 April 1944). She in turn talks of 'finding consolation'
(p. 183), as if Peter is somehow a substitute for something more
satisfying. Even in the middle of her detailed account of their
first real kiss, Anne's mind strays from a simple recollection of
blissful enjoyment to commenting on Peter's need for affection
(p. 182). Their declaration of love, or something like it as symbolized in their recent physical closeness, actually marks the
beginning of Anne's understanding that she and Peter have no
future. The early bubble of infatuated wonder has burst, and
without its distracting influence, Anne is able to write with courage and insight about Peter's failings (p. 183). Over two years his
junior, she sees very clearly the distance between them, the
absence in Peter of the qualities she values most highly in herself. (Compare for example the end of the entry for 11 April in
which Anne declares her own hopes, with what she now feels
about Peter.) Her new realization is supported by her father,
who comments independently about Peter's weak character (p.
185), and also immediately afterwards by the naïve nature of
Peter's comments as he and Anne discuss her talk with Pim.

Towards the end of the section (19 May), there is a clear
example of the ambivalence Anne now displays when writing
about Peter. On the one hand, she assures herself that everything is fine – what a difference of tone when compared with,
say, the entry for 28 April – but then refers dismissively to Peter
as 'the poor boy'. Further, she affirms her love and affection for
him, but in the same breath seems almost relieved that he no

longer has access to her deepest thoughts and feelings (p. 196). Perhaps one explanation lies in her use of 'my love', which seems to indicate the condition of being in love, of whispered conversations and close contact, and which is distinct from the love derived from shared attitudes and hopes of a profound nature.

Another sign of Anne's growing dissatisfaction with Peter can be seen in the structure of this section. He does not dominate the entries to quite the same extent as in the last two sections, and there is the sense that Anne is determined to turn to other subjects. There is a long period from 8 to 16 May in which Peter's only appearance is to mop up after the incontinent Mouschi (p. 193), and even this episode relegates him while most attention is given to the cat. Really, apart from the brief and no-nonsense comments about Peter in the entry for 19 May, he disappears very sharply from the section after Anne's resolution to turn over a new leaf (p. 190). It is as if Anne feels that as part of her decision to 'take Daddy as my example' (p. 190), she must turn to many new subjects for her diary in order to put her relationship with Peter into a proper perspective. She descriptively returns to familiar territory and safe emotional ground – her parents' backgrounds and Miep's story of a party (8 May), Mrs Van Daan's obtuseness (9 May), her studies (11 May), Pim's birthday (13 May), a vividly scripted account of another of the Van Daans' rows (16 May), and a humorous description of when her papers were accidentally soaked. This long sequence of relatively trivial entries, written perhaps to divert herself from thinking excessively about Peter, gives way at the end of the section to a long discussion about international loyalties and anti-Semitism; the latter has now begun to find expression amongst the Dutch, formerly close allies of the Jews.

Anne writes with common sense about attitudes to the British (p. 198) and with an understandable despair about the future should the German Jews who sought sanctuary in Holland be forced to return home. Her indignant defence of her race is apparent in the series of rhetorical questions (p. 199) and in her recitation of the Jewish slogan that delineates the different responsibilities carried by Jews and Gentiles. She shows a mature and intelligent grasp of the issues and, as before, affirms her love of Holland.

The section closes with the further bad news that their greengrocer, a helpful ally, has been arrested, and we notice that while

Anne obviously refers to the increased difficulties this will mean for the annexe, her first thought (p. 200) is for their friend. The episode ends with a recognition that no matter what their hardships, the main issue is still to avoid discovery at all costs.

Glossary Section 11

p. 191 **hors d'oeuvre** A light savoury to whet the appetite before a main meal.

p. 192 **Ellen the fairy** Published as 'The Fairy' in *Tales from the Secret Annexe*.

p. 193 **Gerbrandy** Dutch Prime Minister.

p. 194 *Galilei* Galileo Galilei was an eminent Italian astronomer and physicist (1564–1642), famous for, amongst other things, his velocity experiment from the leaning tower of Pisa.

p. 194 **The Emperor Charles V** Nephew of Catherine of Aragon, King of Spain, Burgundy and the Netherlands, elected Holy Roman Emperor (1519–1556).

p. 194 **Theseus ... Hercules** All prominent figures in Greek mythology.

p. 194 **Myron and Phidias** Famous Greek sculptors of the ancient world.

p. 194 **Seven and Nine Years' Wars** Wars between Spain and the Netherlands.

p. 194 **the bathing Suzanna** See Daniel xiii.

p. 194 **Sodom and Gomorrah** See Genesis xix.

p. 195 **Linnaeus** Carolus Linnaeus (1708–78) Swedish naturalist, founder of modern botany.

p. 195 **the Atlantic Wall** German U-boat defence installations, gun emplacements, etc. along the western coast of France to help consolidate their control of western Europe.

p. 197 **Maria de Medici** Properly Maria de' Medici (1573–1642) a member of the famous Italian family. Consort of Henry IV of France 1600–1610.

p. 197 **William of Orange** Late seventeenth-century Dutch king who became King of England in 1688.

p. 197 **Marie Antoinette** (1755–1793) Consort of Louis XVI of France.

p. 200 **The girls ... aren't allowed** Miep and Elli were not allowed to do heavy shopping.

Section 12 26 May 1944–1 August 1944

Anne's growing disenchantment with Peter finds clear expression in this section as part of a wider statement of self-analysis and understanding. She is caught in a tension which arises for a number of reasons, and finds herself in the difficult position of having to review her feelings for him while still needing desperately the type of emotional contact that he provides. The tension is that of conflicting demands of heart and mind. On the one hand, Anne is a young girl, barely fifteen, who for some two years has been denied access to the normal range of interests and activities for someone of her age. Undoubtedly the popular, lively thirteen-year-old who started this diary would in normal circumstances have filled her time with outings, dances, boyfriends, clubs and a host of other social involvements. It is unlikely that the quiet, introverted Peter Van Daan would ever have caught her attention if they had not been forced to live in the imposed intimacy of the annexe. However, the parallel needs of a close friend in whom she could confide, a member of the opposite sex with whom she could begin to explore the conventions and possibilities of a romantic relationship, and an affinity with someone outside her family, understandably resulted in her turning to Peter. Although he was uncertain and unfamiliar with Anne's world of wit and words, he was pleasant, courageous, good-looking and sympathetic. We have already seen the steady growth of their friendship, accompanied by an inevitable move towards a physical expression of their affection.

Throughout Section 11 however, and with increasing force and direction in this one, Anne begins to comprehend the true nature of what she has called their love. Even before we read the substantial and lucid insights into Peter's nature (14 June, 6 July and 15 July), Anne refers again on 13 June to him as 'the poor boy'. (See also 19 May 1944.) The term reveals a definite assumption about their relative positions, and we receive the clear impression that Peter no longer has any ability to earn Anne's admiration. She writes the next day, however, of her need to see Peter as frequently as she can, but is very aware of two major deficiencies in his character which preclude the possibility of a more complete friendship. Firstly, her feeling that Peter sees her 'not as a lover but as a friend' (p. 207) stems from her reluctant acceptance of his incommunicative and passive nature; she laments rather than resents his inability to share his inner thoughts with her, and yearns for a time when he will respond to her in the way she needs.

Secondly, Peter seems to have inherited something of his

parents' superficiality. Anne refers (14 June) to his hostility to religious practice and his excessive interest in food and other uninteresting things. As we know, while not strictly orthodox Jews, the Franks had a fundamental faith in God and saw their religion as an essential part of their lives. Writing on 6 July, Anne (referring again to Peter as a 'poor boy') spells out his lack of religious commitment and sees it as a symbol of his lack of inner resources. In contrast to Anne's fierce determination to 'work and do good', and her awareness that 'laziness may appear attractive, but work gives satisfaction' (p. 212), Peter seems satisfied to let life slide by on a path of easy choices and trivial matters.

The difference between them is very forcefully declared in the same entry, when Anne contrasts 'a type like Peter' with 'a conscious living being' (p. 212). This is an unambiguous, painful and even scathing reference to Peter's inadequacies, and it marks the death of Anne's hopes for a new beginning.

The last reference to Peter is an epitaph of their relationship (15 July, p. 217). Anne changes from using the present tense when referring to Pim, to the past tense for Peter. She realizes the idealized picture of him she had built up because of her need for 'a living person to whom I could pour out my heart' and regrets the intimacy she allowed to develop. Characteristically, she accepts the responsibility for their fruitless attachment, and even her understanding of his parasitic need for her (p. 218) is only stated in the context of her wish to help him to be more independent. Her last sentence about Peter is not written by a lover, or even a close friend, but by a caring adult about a feckless teenager.

Anne's bravely realistic appraisal of her friendship with Peter is part of a penetrating analysis of herself – her character, the impression she makes on others, the reasons for her apparent misbehaviour, her attitudes, her 'self-consciousness' (p. 216). This section contains a number of entries in which she reflects at length about these profound inner matters. Without these entries, the diary would be seriously impoverished, for, despite the unhappy uncertainty in the closing lines, there is a sense of completeness created by Anne's lucid understanding of her own nature. She has not achieved peace or contentment – who at her age and in her situation could have? She does, however, understand clearly the nature of her difficulties, and examines them with a comprehensive and perceptive vision from which all illusion has been excised.

For all her independence, as the youngest member of the annexe refugees Anne felt keenly the constant nagging and correction she was subject to throughout the twenty-five months spent there. Mrs Van Daan, 'one of my chief accusers' (p. 206) clashes frequently with Anne, who finds it difficult to tolerate fools gladly. The third paragraph for 14 June succinctly lists her failings, the principal one seeming to be hypocrisy – or blindness to her own faults. It should be noted though that Mrs Van Daan really functions in a semi-comic role, as a sort of elder ugly sister to Anne's Cinderella. The tone of the comments about Mrs Van Daan's general nagging (9 June) is of good-humoured long-suffering; Anne's wistful scheme of punishment robs her words of any malice or anger. She had obviously come to realize that Mrs Van Daan was not a worthy opponent (16 June) and sought relief in laughter rather than retaliation.

She is able too to view objectively the causes of friction between her and her mother. The earlier realization of the huge emotional distance between them has been identified and accepted, and Anne directs no criticism at her. What she does do is to criticize herself (14 June) in her constant search for improvement; we can only wonder at the desperate self-restraint which, even after two years' confinement, still keeps her looking to the future and hoping for the special person who will bring out the best in her.

The long entry for 6 July addresses this question of her determination to improve. Using Peter as a comparison to herself, Anne's views about the value of work in contrast to 'a lazy deceitful life' are polarized in what some might see as a statement of relentlessly Victorian values. Again however, we need to remember for how long they were all thrown upon their own resources, and how Anne had two contrasting examples to follow – the creative, industrious practice of her parents, particularly her father's and the shameless exhibitions of bad temper and selfishness displayed by Peter's parents, especially Mrs Van Daan. Given a choice between these extremes, it is not surprising that Anne followed the positive example and rejected the negative one. Her decisiveness is seen in the uncompromising analysis and imagery of 'How can I make it clear ... to raise onself?' (p. 212).

Her religious views are also stated in this entry. She admits to not being an orthodox Jew, and in the final paragraph she dismisses the transcendental aspects of her faith. What is important to her is the practical matter 'of upholding ... one's ... conscience' (p. 212). The paragraph is not an informed comment about the complex question of religious belief, but a series of moralistic platitudes which, for all their naïvety, confirm the stength of Anne's industrious approach to life.

Although much of her time was devoted to reading and study, Anne also felt it important to keep abreast of the latest war news. She naturally based her hopes of liberty on a successful Allied forces' invasion of Europe and makes several references to invasion news (6, 9, 13, 23, 27, 30 June, 21 July). In addition to the confident, detailed grasp of the subject matter, no doubt culled from the adults' conversation, there is the enthusiasm that accompanies each entry. Each new development becomes the springboard for an expression of hope, and is seized on by Anne to counteract the prevalent atmosphere of despondency caused by the lack of food, the domestic privations, and the cumulative effect of two years' confinement (26 May). An idea of Anne's depressed condition at this time is given by her hostile reaction to the devoted Miep's present (p. 201). In addition to these difficulties shared with her seven companions, Anne is unhappy about her relationships, principally with Peter, but also with her father.

As has been the case with her mother and Peter, Anne feels that her rejection of her father (p. 217) is provoked by what she perceives as his failure to gain her deepest confidence. By a process of question and answer, or conclusion followed by explanation, Anne examines how she has grown away from her father (15 July), and then considers the question of whether youth suffers more than age (p. 218). Her answer that the exigencies of the evil all around them destroy the possibility of sustained ideals is clearly and potently argued. On a more personal level she articulates in the prophetic language of other great fighters for freedom, such as Martin Luther King and Nelson Mandela, her resolution to follow her ideals in the face of 'the ever-approaching thunder' (p. 218).

Although international and personal matters account for most of this section, Anne still finds time to relate day-to-day events in the annexe. Her entry for 31 May reminds us of her talent for mimicry, and we see again on 8 July how well she can transpose a domestic chore into a lively story through dialogue, exaggeration, description and humorous commentary.

The last entry of the section (1 August 1944) is a long, honest assessment of herself, and is therefore a fitting conclusion to the diary. She reiterates her awareness of her 'dual personality' (p. 220), and we sense only too clearly the inner turmoil she suffered.

As always, the clarity and depth of her thought are remarkable. True to her ideals, she looks for no easy answers in this letter. Instead, she charges herself with the responsibility for her own failings and never attempts to blame them on the impossible life she has lived for over two years. The passage is particularly important as she clears away any misunderstanding about herself.

Anne's diary has been translated into dozens of languages, has been an international bestseller for years, and has inspired the creation of a centre for racial and religious freedom. Anne Frank has in death been one of this century's most powerful voices for tolerance and international cooperation.

In the light of this achievement, her closing words are tragically ironic; she sees herself as having the capacity to do good, 'if ... there weren't any other people living in the world.'

Glossary Section 12

p. 203 **Fifth Army** General Mark Clark led the US 5th Army into Italy in the autumn of 1943 with the British 8th Army. By June of the following year they had captured Rome from German and Italian troops.

p. 203 **Pas de Calais** N. E. France, around Calais extending down to Arras.

p. 203 **D-day** The long promised invasion of northern Europe, the earlier invasion of Italy having been bogged down in the Alps: Allied forces landed in Normandy and established a bridgehead to invade Nazi-occupied Europe (6 June 1944).

p. 203 **Calais, Boulogne, Le Havre and Cherbourg** French northern channel ports.

p. 203 **trial landing like Dieppe** Disastrous amphibious attack in August 1942 by the Allies, mainly Canadian forces, to test the strength of the German defences.

p. 203 **General Dwight Eisenhower** (1890–1969) Supreme

Commander of the Allied Expeditionary Force (1943–1945).

p. 204 **De Gaulle of France** General Charles de Gaulle (1890–1970), Head of the Provisional Government of France (1944–1946), first president of the Fifth Republic.

p. 204 **The King of England** King George VI (1895–1962).

p. 204 **Churchill** Winston Churchill (1874–1965), Prime Minister of the wartime coalition government in Britain (1940–1945).

p. 204 **Caen** Regional capital of Normandy. Site of a protracted siege by the Allies. Devastated by very heavy bombing.

p. 205 **Franz Liszt** (1811–1886) celebrated Hungarian romantic composer.

p. 205 **Schumann ... Mendelssohn** This list contains prominent figures in European music and literature in the nineteenth century.

Schumman Robert Schumann (1810–1856) German composer.

Clara Wieck (1819–1896) Maiden name of Schumann's wife. Formerly a pianist and composer in her own right.

Hector Berlioz Innovative French composer (1803–1869).

Johannes Brahms German romantic composer, in love with Clara Wieck (1833–1897).

Beethoven Ludwig van Beethoven, German composer. Established change from Mozartian classicism to German Romanticism as typified by Liszt, Brahms and Schumann (1770–1827).

Joachim Joseph Joachim, Hungarian violinist and composer, friend of Brahms who wrote many violin works for him (1831–1907).

Richard Wagner German composer of massive operas, principally the Ring cycle, *Tristan and Isolde* and the *Mastersingers from Nurnberg* (1813–1883).

Hans Von Bülow German virtuoso pianist and conductor: married Liszt's daughter (1830–1894).

Anton Rubinstein Russian pianist and composer (1829–1894).

Frédéric Chopin Polish virtuoso pianist and composer of many innovative piano works (1810–1849).

Victor Hugo French poet and novelist. Famous for *Notre Dame de Paris* and *Les Misérables*. Leader of French Romantic movement (1802–1885).

Honoré de Balzac Eminent French novelist. Author of *La Comédie Humaine*, a collection of romances which aim to represent the whole panoply of French society. A great and influential author (1799–1850).

Hiller and **Hummel** Either Ferdinand (1811–1885) or Johann (1728–1804) Hiller; Johann Nepomuk Hummel (1778–1837): minor German composers.

Czerny Karl Czerny, Viennese pianist and composer who studied under Beethoven and taught Liszt (1791–1857).

Rossini Gioacchimo Rossini, great Italian operatic composer, famous for *The Barber of Seville* and the *Stabat Mater* (1792–1868).

Cherubini Maria Cherubini, Italian composer of operatic and instrumental works (1760–1842).

Paganini Nicolo Paganini, the virtuoso violinist: the brilliance of his playing gave rise to speculation that he was in league with the Devil (1782–1840).

Mendelssohn Felix Mendelssohn, German composer famous for symphonies and incidental music. Responsible for the revival of interest in Bach's music in Germany (1809–1847).

p. 206 **Maria Theresa** Maria Theresa, the wife of Francis I, an eighteenth-century Emperor of the Holy Roman Empire. Noted for her vigour and remarkable strength of character and ability. Clearly someone from whom Anne would have drawn great inspiration (1717–1780).

p. 206 **Smuts** General Jan Christian Smuts, South African statesman and Prime Minister 1939–1948.

p. 206 **Arnold** General Henry 'Hap' Arnold, close colleague of Eisenhower in D-day invasion plans.

p. 209 **Vitebsk** A Russian town, south-west of Moscow, near Polish border.

p. 210 **Slobin** A town in south-western Russia, north-west of Kiev.

p. 210 **Cotentin Peninsula** In north-western Normandy, centred on Cherbourg.

p. 210 **'V-weapon'** German V-1 'Doodlebugs', unmanned jet-propelled flying bombs unleashed against England in 1944.

p. 210 **Boche, Bocheland** Slang, offensive reference to Germans and Germany.

p. 210 **Bolsheviks** The ruling Communist party in the Soviet Union from 1917 onwards.

p. 210 **Groningen, Friesland and Gelderland** Towns in northern Netherlands.

p. 211 **An Ideal Husband** A play by the Irish writer Oscar Wilde (1854–1900).

p. 211 **Bobruisk, Mogilev and Orsha** Towns on the river Dnepr in western Russia, south-west of Moscow.

p. 213 **Beverwijk** A town near Amsterdam.

p. 219 **An attempt has been made on Hitler's life** An assassination attempt was made by German officers under the leadership of Claus von Stauffenberg on 6 July 1944.

p. 220 **little Johnnie** An unflattering reference to German infantry.

Assignments Sections 11 and 12

1 Following assignment 4, sections 5 and 6, trace from section 7 mentions of the Van Daans to the end of the diary. Note any

change in the frequency of such entries and also in Anne's attitude to the Van Daans. Give reasons why such changes might have occurred.

2 Anne and Peter spent a great deal of time in each other's company. After a while, Anne became discontented with Peter's lack of conversation. Try scripting for radio (i.e. sound only) what you might see as a typical evening's talk between them at that time, i.e. developments in the war, domestic issues, problems with adults or anything else that might have concerned them so as to bring out their different characters.

3 Both sections contain long passages of reflection on Anne's nature. Write an account of her attitude to herself and those around her. Identify what you feel are the main sources of (a) her inner unhappiness and (b) her aims in life.

Anne Frank's art in the *Diary*

The characters

Anne Frank

I have lots of courage, I always feel so strong and as if I can bear a great deal, I feel so free and so young!

The dominant impression we gain of Anne Frank from her diary is of youth, optimism, strength, courage and determination. Despite very natural times of despair, her resolve to survive and to win remains firm, and it is cruelly ironic that she should have been arrested shortly after writing the above lines.

The diary shows her change from a girl into a young woman of exceptional courage and ability. She starts as a social butterfly, a happy-go-lucky, popular, mildly flirtatious thirteen-year-old (sections 1, 4), and develops into someone who has been through a cathartic experience which has modified her natural qualities (9–12).

She has a sharp, quick mind (2, 3, 4, 6), to the dismay of her adult companions, but gains a profound ability to look into herself and others (3, 5, 9–12) especially Peter (7, 8, 9). Her awareness of her moral and intellectual superiority to him does not, however, result in arrogance, only in disappointment (11, 12). She has a real desire to improve her nature (8, 10–12), and invidious comparisons cannot play a part in her scheme of things.

Her commitment to study and hard work reflects her deep desire to achieve real good in the world (10, 12). She rejects the traditional role of a woman and trains herself rigorously for the life that was denied her (3, 10, 11). The time spent in the annexe was clearly worse for her than for Peter or Margot (2, 5, 6, 11): she refers to their lack of life, and we sense her frustration at their confined existence.

Her constant theme is her lack of an intimate equal. It is the reason why the diary exists, and through the absence of such a companion and the consequent commitment to paper of what might have been lost in conversation, we are left with a permanent account of her development. For example, the process by which she falls in and out of love with Peter is movingly recorded

(1, 4, 5, 7, 8, 9, 12). She uses the diary as an emotional and intellectual sounding board, confiding to it her deepest joys and worries, and gaining strength from the habit of deep reflection that it encourages.

Otto Frank (Pim)

He is the one I look up to. I don't love anyone in the world but him.

Well into middle age, Otto Frank had just embarked on a second major adjustment to his life and that of his family when Anne wrote the above words. Having fled Germany to avoid anti-Jewish hostility in the 1930s to settle in Amsterdam, he was then forced to hide his family, with that of a colleague, and another Jewish man. Further, he decided to sign away the controlling interest in his business and had to abandon his comfortable suburban home in Amsterdam.

He did not respond to this second series of setbacks by surrendering. Instead, he kept up an active involvement in his former companies, found time to teach Anne, and stepped into the role of leader and peace-maker in the annexe. He was determined not to succumb to the fresh blows of losing his home, to the threat to himself and his family and to the daily friction in the annexe. We appreciate that Anne did not only look up to and love him, but saw him as an example for her own life.

He is a slightly shadowy figure, benevolent, but not usually in close focus. He is referred to as a sort of arbiter of Anne's happiness or unhappiness and this comparative lack of attention is curious. Given her admiration for her father, why did Anne not present him more fully? The probable reason lay in his natural reserve and modesty. Unlike the Van Daans, he was simply not the sort of person who could be written about in a vigorous way. Even the long entry for 15 July 1944 in which Anne examines why Pim failed to help her through her difficult period of rebelliousness only presents him as a kind man who had taken the wrong approach with her. Her loyalty and love for him precludes any critical account, and he remains in our minds the gentlemanly, caring man who quite rightly 'avoids all arguments about Mummy' (5 January 1944). He was in his quiet way an essential part of Anne's life – a teacher, friend, an undoubted influence for good.

Edith Frank

I can't really love Mummy in a dependent child-like way – I just don't have that feeling.

Although some fourteen months pass between Anne's enthusiastic affirmation of love for her father and the contrasting words above, her attitude never really changes. The entry for 24 December 1943 is a telling examination of the function of pet names and reveals again the emotional distance between Edith Frank and Anne. (See also the distressing incident recorded on 2 April 1943.)

Although a cultured woman, Edith Frank appears not to have the imaginative knack of being able to get alongside her demanding younger daughter, whose quick intelligence soon sees through what had become an empty relationship. Anne rejects the conventional, domestic range of achievements which appear to satisfy her mother and is thus intellectually and emotionally isolated from her. No anger is apparent and Anne comes to terms with their distanced situation and shows no real resentment towards her mother. However, she sees herself as superior to her and limits her presence in the diary to an occasional comment.

Margot

I do know that she shares my feelings over most things.

Intellectually, Margot is close to Anne. They share the same bookish interests and Anne clearly respects her elder sister's academic achievements. Although fond of Margot and able to discuss important things with her, Anne can never be entirely satisfied with her conformist attitude to life (5 February 1943). Margot lacks the imaginative energy which is so much a part of Anne's nature. The infrequent references to her are more like duty visits than enthusiastic memories. We can only feel sad that the one person near Anne's age with similar intellectual tastes to hers could not be the close companion she so wanted.

Herman and Petronella Van Daan; Albert Dussel

Mr Van Daan: 'Self-satisfaction' has reached a high grade with this gentleman.

Mrs Van Daan: She is the guilty one in all the arguments.
Dr Dussel: Helps himself, never looks up, eats and doesn't talk.

The Van Daans are caricatured, noisy, larger-than-life adult intruders into Anne Frank's world of books and study. They introduce her to extremes of emotional indulgence and are contrasted directly with her parents.

Mrs Van Daan incurs most criticism for her moodiness, her flirting, her vanity and her unfairness, the last of which was often directed at Anne, who resented it keenly.

She is rescued however from any serious suggestion of malignancy in two ways. Humour is often used to lampoon her more ridiculous actions, and this then paves the way for Anne to concede, very occasionally, that her favourite enemy does have one or two good points. Anne writes without scorn of how she cares for Mrs Van Daan, who is petrified following the burglary (11 April 1944). This implies that Anne's dislike is superficial and, correspondingly, that Mrs Van Daan's faults are irritating rather than evil.

Her husband is at once a more robust presence and a less interesting subject for Anne's pen. He is pompous, greedy and short-tempered, rowing with his wife, Peter, and even the peaceful Otto Frank. Again, however, Anne's presentation of him is tempered with good humour, and she delights in the sausage-making scene in which we suspect Van Daan enjoyed his prominent role.

As with his wife and Dussel, Van Daan is really only prominent in the first half of the diary. As Anne becomes interested in larger affairs, so his trivial misdemeanours are relegated to their correct place.

Dr Dussel is a figure of fun. The summarized character outline (9 August 1943) is drawn with a Dickensian flair for the gross and the ridiculous, as is the account of his bedtime preparations (4 August 1943). His greed and passion for cigarettes dominate Anne's presentation of him, and even the extended account of his selfishness over the shared use of his and Anne's room may be exaggerated. Anne is indignant rather than angry, and relishes the opportunity to dismiss her room-mate as 'frightfully childish'.

Peter Van Daan

Although Peter is obviously an important figure, especially in the second half of the diary, so much time has been spent examining him and his relationship with Anne in sections 8 to 123 that only a brief summary is needed now.

As the only boy in the annexe, he was forced into an isolated situation. This, coupled with his naturally uncommunicative nature and a keen sense of embarrassment about himself and his parents, made him in some senses the perfect figure for Anne to idealize into the kindred spirit she craved.

His lack of character is indicated not only through Anne's overt disappointment in him, but also through the general absence of any accounts of conversations or shared activities.

Peter's role in Anne's development is, as we come to realize, a means by which she can measure the nature of her emotional needs. Even though she finds him lacking, he has given her an essential insight into her own nature and as such he has been a valuable part of her childhood.

Setting

The diary started on Sunday 14 June 1942, just after Anne's thirteenth birthday. Exactly twenty-five months had passed since Germany completed its invasion of Holland, and although Dutch Jews had been forced to bow to increasingly stringent conditions imposed by the Nazi authorities, it was still possible for them to live a relatively normal life.

Less than one month later, the Franks and Van Daan, later followed by Dussel, were flung into a secret life which lasted for a further twenty-five months. They were trapped inside a three-hundred-year-old building at 263 Prinsengracht, Amsterdam, the premises of the grocery business that Otto Frank had prudently signed over to his Christian colleagues. Careful study of the map on p. 26 of the Pan edition shows how small the accommodation was for eight people, three of them teenagers.

The building was damp – its front faces a canal – and the upper floors where the refugees hid had previously been used to store the clutter from the business below. Access to the 'annexe', as Anne called it, was via a doorway, cleverly concealed by an opening bookcase designed by the father of a typist employed by the companies.

Sleeping, washing, toilet and eating arrangements were cramped and at times unbearable. Anne shared a room with Dussel, Margot shared with her parents, and the Van Daans had a bedroom on the top floor (which was also used as a general dining/living room) adjacent to a tiny corridor room used by Peter.

The claustrophobic conditions made the practical aspects of living together very difficult; the emotional consequences were also very trying. The near complete absence of privacy and the constant strain of having to keep quiet were particularly difficult for Anne, who felt keenly the denial of space and fresh air – look up the various references to her longing for contact with nature.

It is a tribute to the faithful support of their friends and colleagues that they kept alive and relatively well during their stay. Food and other essentials were in short supply in Holland, and providing for eight people without drawing attention to oneself was a difficult and dangerous business.

There was much to contend with – burglars, rats, bad plumbing, the cold, the damp – in addition to the usual daily difficulties. Poor health was to be feared, as there was no chance of getting to a doctor, and opportunities for exercise were naturally limited. There was no natural light as the windows had to be blacked out for fear of discovery.

The refugees were however fortunate in that they had regular contact with their trusted friends and colleagues. They also had access to a radio which gave them comfort via broadcasts from the BBC.

The irony of *The Diary of Anne Frank* is that without this situation it would obviously never have been written. Anne would certainly have kept an interesting and amusing diary, but it would have remained at that level. The cramped cell of the annexe made for creative sharpness. In creating the most famous plea for tolerance and freedom that we are likely to see, Anne in the annexe symbolizes the hope that people lived for, that truth and goodness will triumph over oppression.

. **Themes**

It is necessary to remember the sporadic, moody impetus behind Anne's writing. She wrote to reflect on various matters, to describe scenes and to entertain herself. It would be more accurate to refer to 'issues' rather than 'themes', as indicated in the contents page.

There are several types of issue. One is to do with the events that arose in the annexe – anything from mouldy potatoes to an incontinent cat – which caught Anne's attention or which she felt would provide material for a descriptive or anecdotal account. She is excellent at breathing life into the most unlikely subjects and the diary is not impoverished because of such concerns. Indeed, her humorous portrayal of such apparently trivial things as an outbreak of fleas (3 August 1943) serves to remind us of the indignities and inconveniences the group was exposed to.

Relationships are an important focus for Anne's pen. There are many moments of frustration and anger prompted largely by Anne's conflict with Mrs Van Daan, although Mr Van Daan, Dussel, her mother and even her father come in for their share of criticism. Disputes arise and are recorded over such little things as the relative sizes of portions of margarine – and again, we remember the constant possibility of friction arising from cramped accommodation and the underlying threat of discovery.

The most significant relationship is of course between Anne and Peter, and it occupies a large part of the second half of the diary. It eventually provides Anne with an insight into her own nature, the understanding of which is another dominant aspect of the diary. Self-understanding is of great importance to Anne. She talks on 15 July 1944 of her 'self-consciousness', her 'knowledge of myself'. It is fuelled by her need for a special person with whom she can share the things that matter most to her and is a natural condition for someone of her intelligence, cultured background and passion for literature. She sees herself as 'a conscious living being' (6 July 1944). For her one of the purposes of living is to probe beneath the surface of her life and question the influences and motives that govern her thoughts and behaviour.

Related to this habit of calling her inner being to attention is her passionate commitment to work, to train and prepare herself for a life dedicated to doing good. Inevitably, her race, her present situation and her background are all agents in her desire to improve the world, and her despairing indignation about the fate of the Jews leads us to another area of the diary. Although not an orthodox Jew, Anne's faith is clearly very important to her; she sees religious belief as conditional to a living faith in people (Peter's scepticism is one reason why she becomes disillusioned with him) and feels a tremendous solidarity with the huge numbers of Jews who were consigned to death camps.

War news is the last major area in the diary. Anne's intelligence quickly grasps the key people, places and operations of the war in Europe, and she is able to make spirited and informed comments about them. As does everyone, she waits fervently for Hitler's defeat – and preferably, his death – and laments the low state to which the world has been brought by his oppressive dictatorship.

The issues with which Anne deals are predictable given her situation. It is her treatment of them – sensitive, moving, intelligent, evocative writing – which sets her diary in the front rank of its genre.

Structure

The basic facts of the book's structure have already been established. It has a hundred and seventy-three entries, from Sunday 14 June 1942 to Tuesday 1 August 1944, a period which approximately covers Anne's thirteenth to her fifteenth birthdays. Its organization is determined very much by the demands of its subject matter.

The first half of the diary, to the end of 1943, is mainly concerned with what might loosely be called general annexe matters – settling in, details of their new home, their companions, the endless details of daily living. Soon, the ticklish matter of conflicts between personalities starts to dominate Anne's interest, and she readily sets to work to describe the foibles of her companions, especially Mrs Van Daan.

Nothing is too insignificant for her at this stage; she moves fluidly from cats to food, from nagging adults to her latest reading. She is still young enough to be able to lose herself in portraying the more superficial aspects of life in the annexe and clearly gains some largely innocent enjoyment from her sketches of the peculiarities of Dussel and the Van Daans.

The other half of the book is taken up by the eighty-six entries for 1944. There are three main reasons why this is so. Firstly, Anne's relationship with Peter occupies her thoughts to a great extent. It starts definitely with her decision to talk with him (6 January), progresses through a brief period of glorious infatuation and then dies slowly as she realizes that Peter will never bring her the true satisfaction she seeks.

The next important area is that of war news. Although it does not occupy the same space as the other two, there is considerable coverage given to new developments despite Anne's disparaging remarks about what she sees as the adults' excessive interest in politics (27 March). Her own maturity, however, stimulates a growing awareness of the importance of political/military news and her imagination is caught by the growing hope of an Allied invasion. She reflects dispassionately and at length on the merits of the Dutch (22 May) and on the larger issues of anti-Semitism and international conflict.

The last main concern is herself – not egotistically – but for self-discovery. She is fully aware of the processes of her own mind and she presents them in a comprehensive and ordered fashion; the long entries for 15 July and 1 August are remarkable exercises in introspection.

As there is no underlying pattern which directs the diary, structure is best seen as a label which describes (a) the chronological division which operates at the start of 1944, and (b) the issues which receive renewed attention from time to time.

Style

Unlike a planned piece of unified writing, a diary is unpredictable and random, unlimited by any need to conform to what has gone before or is to come.

It is still possible however to make a number of observations about the style of *The Diary of Anne Frank*, as it recirculates and recapitulates on a number of themes. These tend inevitably to be dictated by life in the annexe and by Anne's own development. It must, however, be borne in mind that any comments about style are made in the knowledge that we are reading a translation; conclusions about Anne's attitudes, talents and so on must therefore be made cautiously.

The first thing to say is that Anne loves using words. This is not as obvious as it may seem, for many diaries are filled with uninspired or overwritten clutter, or are limited to a record of mundane events. In contrast, every page of Anne's diary reveals the presence of a gifted writer. A variety of matters is handled easily and lightly, with frequent pauses for the writer to pass a comment on her subject.

The diary starts in much the same way as any other; it is filled with newsy, chatty snippets of day-to-day information, but even these are enlivened by vivid comments and character sketches; for example, that of Mr Keptor, the teacher who amicably crossed swords with Anne because of her persistent talking in class. Her writing often has the same quality of spontaneous, vivid conversation in which a subject is picked up and deftly examined before a new one is found.

There is a noticeable change of approach following the arrival of Margot's call-up notice. Although there is still much chat and humour, the new element of danger inevitably overshadows Anne's thoughts and much attention is paid to annexe life, the war and her own feelings.

Whatever the subject matter, whether frivolous or sombre, there are certain common aspects of style which should be noted. The use of exclamations is a common enough device in the personal writing of young people, and Anne uses it to denote both excitement and indignation. The marks are used sparingly, not to stimulate artificially a dull piece of writing, but to complete the effect of something that is intrinsically lively.

Similarly, her frequent use of question marks stamps her work with an air of natural enquiry. She considers an issue and the punctuation indicates the process of a lively debate. Her use of punctuation reflects her total engagement with writing.

Much mention has already been made of her use of dialogue. She remembers the general drift of what has been said and perhaps even a few lines of it. She then takes these recollections and uses them as a basis for a written conversation, often abstaining from any authorial intervention. This has the result of giving a very natural feel to the dialogue; the characters – including herself at times – speak for themselves and often become the cast of a domestic comedy, as with the episode of the Van Daans' row about air raids (18 August 1943).

More serious subjects are handled with a similar facility.

Tense moments (Margot's call-up, the burglary) read like thril-lers. Atmospheres are described through searching descriptions of silence, sudden sounds and tense expressions. Every detail is called into use for the sake of the story – a true story – which convinces the reader by recreating the experiences of the writer.

Whatever the subject, Anne writes with a wealth of detail resulting from observation and imagination. Her accounts of people, scenes, her feelings for world events are therefore never bland, but always informed by the adroit use of what she sees, hears and feels.

The organization of Anne's material is obviously governed by what she is interested in. The longer reflective passages of the later parts of the diary are a lesson in structured, cogent writing. There is no maudlin repetition of grievances, but a sincere exposition of her thoughts and feelings, in which the attitudes of other people receive equally keen scrutiny. There is no sense of emotional indulgence, but, rather that of a constant need to search out what is right or true in a situation.

Although Anne never intended her diary for publication, she saw it as a testing ground for the career she wanted to pursue in journalism. Her grasp of what makes a good story is more than apparent here (her creative work lacks the same force) and we are privileged to read the early work of someone who would have reached the highest levels in journalistic or academic writing.

In conclusion, perhaps it ought to be said that the style gives evidence of Anne's own development over the twenty-four months. There is a raciness and colloquial ease throughout – Anne does not hesitate to use clichés which fall readily to hand. But the writing, whether clichéd or otherwise, has the quality of being spontaneous and vital. This is not to say that she does not take care – she does. In a sense, there is evidence of conscient-iousness as well, seen in the detailed information which gives the reader such a full picture of herself and of daily events, whether commonplace, unusual, exciting, humorous or disturbing. And towards the end, with the determined course of reading she undertakes, there is some natural display of names and learning. The style is the girl – observant, responsive, aware: the words light the page with their immediacy of impression, the glow of real life despite the darkness of situation.

General questions plus questions on related topics for coursework/examinations on other books you may be studying

1 In what ways is Anne's independence portrayed in the diary?

Suggested notes for essay answer:
Confides to diary need for special friend, therefore sees herself as alone. Fond of sister, but very different from her and recognizes Margot can never share her ambitions. Emotionally isolated from mother whom she feels has never really shown her affection – rejects mother. Speaks her mind and will not be dominated by adults. Especially so with Mrs Van Daan and Dussel. Keeps innermost thoughts to herself and even excludes father from them (albeit regretfully). Fierce ambition to do something important – will not accept ordinary woman's role – therefore very keen to develop talents – welcomes work. Strong feelings – anger at unjust criticism – e.g. Peter (maintains relationship despite adults' comments). Has to find own answers to problems. Optimistic – determined to laugh at difficulties – lives in hope – will not succumb to despair. Unusual ability to examine her own thoughts and feelings.

2 Would it be fair to label Anne as a rebellious teenager?

3 What are the particular qualities of the diary that have caused it to be such a huge bestseller?

4 Comment on Anne's relationship with her father. Why do you think she was so much closer to him than to her mother?

5 What for you is the most important aspect of the diary? Show how it is presented.

6 To what extent does the diary give a convincing picture of what life was like for Dutch Jews at that time? (History students.)

7 Indicate how Mr and Mrs Van Daan and Dussel are presented. How does their presentation change as the diary progresses? Why?

8 How would you defend the diary against neo-Nazi charges that it is fabricated anti-Fascist propaganda?

9 Why does Anne write so little about her mother and Margot, especially later in the diary?

10 In what ways is religious belief important to Anne?

11 If Anne had been a few years older, in what ways do you think her diary might have been different?

12 Write as detailed a description as you can of the warehouse and the refugees' quarters above. Comment on how the premises must have affected the inhabitants.

13 Examine in detail one entry which you find particularly interesting.

14 'We have never touched on those things that filled, and still fill, my heart and soul' (p. 217). What were the things that Anne longed to share with Peter?

15 Show some of the ways in which Anne Frank uses language. Refer closely to individual entries and quote freely.

Related questions

16 Compare *The Diary of Anne Frank* with another text, true or fictional, in which a young person is at odds with the adult world.

17 The diary gives valuable insights into family life. Compare it with the presentation of childhood in any other book you are studying.

18 What work by another young writer has made such an impression on you? Try Christopher Nolan's *Under the Eye of the Clock*, or any other book you know well.

19 In what sense can the second half of the diary be read as a love story? Compare it with the presentation of a love story in another novel or play.

20 To what extent does the diary function as both a personal and a historical document about the war? Compare, say, with *The Netherlands at War* or *Schindler's Ark* (see *Further reading*).

21 Compare Anne as first-person narrator with any other 'character' who tells a story in his or her own words.

22 The diary is by its nature autobiographical. Compare it with another autobiography, preferably by a woman.

23 For light relief, two fictional diaries you may enjoy are: *The Diary of a Nobody* by George and Weedon Grossmith and *The Sacred Diary of Adrian Plass, aged 37¾* by Adrian Plass. Compare either of these with *The Diary of Anne Frank*.

Further reading

1 Other writing by Anne Frank

Tales from the Secret Annexe (Penguin, 1988). Stories, essays, fables and reminiscences written in hiding.

2 Personal accounts of Holland in the war

Anne Frank Remembered. Miep Gies and Alison Leslie Gold. Written by an intimate friend of the family. Gives much valuable and fascinating information about life during the occupation.
(Bantam Press, 1987)

Corrie ten Boom: Her Life, Her Faith. Carole C. Carlson.
Biography of a famous Dutch Christian. Chapter 8 – 'God help Holland . . . and Us' – is especially relevant.
(Kingsway Publications Ltd, 1983)

3 Reference works

The Diary of Anne Frank – The Critical Edition
Prepared by the Netherlands State Institute for War Documentation, this is the definitive scholarly edition of over seven hundred pages. Includes the original manuscript, Anne's edited version, and the final version based on alterations made by Otto Frank and his friends. Valuable articles on the Franks' family background, their move to Holland, the arrest, the subsequent inquiry into how they had been discovered, conditions in the concentration camps, the eventual publication of the diary, attacks on the authenticity of the diary and even a detailed study of Anne's handwriting. Hard going, but rewarding for the serious student.
(Viking Penguin, 1989)

The Netherlands at War: 1940–1945. Walter B. Maass.
Historical study of the German occupation of Holland. Rich in detail and very readable. Excellent background information.
(Abelard–Schuman, 1970)

The Lion Rampant. The story of Holland's resistance to the Nazis. L. de Jong and Joseph W. F. Stoppelman.
Contemporary account of Holland's suffering in the Second World War. Lengthy, but valuable if used selectively.
(Querido, 1943)

Churban. The Murder of the Jews of Europe. Tony Bayfield.
School textbook which concentrates on essential information. Much
photographic material. Succinct and readable 'attempt to enable young
people to respond to a shattering episode in Jewish history'.
(The Michael Goulston Educational Foundation, 1981)

Mein Kampf. Adolf Hitler.
Read the excellent introduction by D. C. Watt.
(Hutchinson, 1987)

The War Against the Jews. Lucy S. Davidowicz.
(Weidenfeld and Nicolson, 1975)

European History 1848–1945. T.A. Morris.
See chapter 18.
(Unwin Hyman, 1985)

Europe 1880–1945. J. M. Roberts.
See chapter 15.
(Longman, 1972)

4 Biographies

Anne Frank in the World.
(Anne Frank Foundation, 1985)

Anne Frank. Angela Bull.
(Hamilton, 1984)

Anne Frank. Richard Lawrence.
(F. Watts, 1989)

5 Other books of interest

Schindler's Ark. Thomas Keneally.
Story based on real exploits of Oskar Schindler, who rescued large
numbers of Jews from Auschwitz and Birkenau concentration camps.
(Coronet, 1982)

The Anne Frank centre

The Centre was established in 1957 by Otto Frank and a group of prominent citizens of Amsterdam. Its initial aim was to save the premises where he, Anne and the others had hidden. Today the Centre also exists to promote education, and to combat racism and discrimination of any type.

It operates a large international touring exhibition – 'Anne Frank in the World' – and a smaller display for the use of schools and similar organizations. The Centre supplies educational support material appropriate to various ages and interests.

Over half a million visitors come annually to what is now the Anne Frank House at 263 Prinsengracht, the actual site of the annexe. There is also the Anne Frank Centre at Postbus 730, 1000 AS, Amsterdam, which is a resource centre for work on anti-Semitism and racism.

The Anne Frank Educational Trust UK promotes the exhibitions in Britain. Educational support material can be obtained from the UK representative:

Gillian Walnes
Anne Frank Educational Trust UK
PO Box 991
Wimborne
Dorset
BG21 2YH
Tel: 0202 880305
Fax: 0202 888514